MW01505480

THE
ROYAL
WE

BY RODDY BOTTUM

{ A Memoir }

THE ROYAL WE

BY RODDY BOTTUM

{ A Memoir }

BROOKLYN, NEW YORK
Publishing books since 1997

Published by Akashic Books
©2025 Roddy Bottum

ISBN: 978-1-63614-269-2
Library of Congress Control Number: 2025933492
First printing

EU Authorized Representative details:
Easy Access System Europe
Mustamäe tee 50, 10621 Tallinn, Estonia
gpsr.request@easproject.com

Akashic Books
Brooklyn, New York
Instagram, X, Facebook: AkashicBooks
www.akashicbooks.com
info@akashicbooks.com

1
...

They dared to call it a city.

Not just a city, but *the* city. Hilarious and preposterous but yes. The level of pride from those of us who lived there, in that particular time, was simply profound. The then and there of San Francisco was unique and untouchable. Part of it was the isolation that the geographic provided. She was practically an island, detached from the rest of California by bridges, stretching out on her own, hiding under a shroud of fog, an intellectual bubble. We had no choice but to live there as cocky separatists, crusaders marching and waving our flag, distancing ourselves from the rest of the country.

I'd referred to it from the start as a village.

A city rushes while a village lopes. A city churns while a village percolates. A city tramples and a village tiptoes. The city is a bully who harvests and develops, making big money while the village creates, nestled comfortably in its hijinks, its youth.

Villagers know each other. They intermingle, interact, and bump among themselves in their daily, nodding and acknowledging other villagers as they pass. Shuttling knapsacks and bags, parcels strapped into bike baskets, tubes of rolled-up art projects tucked under arms, baguettes poking out of satchels, purses, and overstuffed sacks, walking, riding, moving at a casual and gentle enough pace to take the time to smile and cock their heads familiarly at their neighbors and merchants and odd street celebrities who pop up again, then again, and again in the mix.

The bearded Santa man marching shirtless up the steepness of Market Street above Castro in denim shorts and boots, always with the red socks; the older identical twins in their sixties, still dressing alike, shopping in Union Square or poised sculpturally side by side on a bus bench; the elegant, well-dressed gentleman with a deep tan and thick head of hair sitting cross-legged, screaming sporadically as the visitors wait in line to board the first cable car at the start of Polk Street; Bambi, Ginger, Dirk, and Tall Paul; Lucifer, Pineapple Head, Carmen the stripper, Cecilia, and Stupid Saul. On and on and on and on, I eventually became one of them, a consuetude among others, an ingredient in the mix, recognizable and regular, a stitch of the fabric, a piece of the quilt. Back when I arrived, though, I knew nothing, and it took forever to become who I was.

It was an accident I went there. I'll never know why I did. I arrived in San Francisco from Los Angeles in 1981 for no reason at all. The only motivation had been to get out of Los Angeles. Los Angeles is a horrible place for children. The sun and the disgusting constancy of weather is a predictable, rotten environment to grow up in. There's a safety and insurance that things won't change and that's detrimental to a growing mind. We learned as children to live in the company of regularity and habit and the constancy of sunny day after sunny day after sunny day. Let's call it oblivious, it still is and I rarely go back. In addition to the fixed conundrum of fetid regularity and false pride is its obsession with beauty. Young people should never clock the importance of a tan, but as children in Los Angeles, we did. We laid out on towels on the lawn in the sun and slathered our bodies in potent lotions from dark plastic bottles, coconut, impossibly oily, working hard to become pretty.

Close on a map but still so far. California is long, from top to bottom, the longest state in the union. A fact I made up but it's feasible, can you see the state in your mind? Los Angeles at the bottom, San Francisco in the middle, and whatever else up top. From the bottom to the middle looked like a short distance but it was far. Four hundred ugly miles from Los Angeles, where I'd grown up and spent my childhood. Ugly, yes, have you driven the 5? It's how I got to San Francisco that first time and then again and again, back and forth on that highway with such regularity that I considered a tattoo of the emblem, the 5 on a badge of blue on my arm, a token of pride for the 400-mile stretch, done again and again.

At first glance, the difference straight up between the two cities was the shock of the weather. As pedantic as that, a change in the weather. Los Angeles is a desert, dry and arid, never not parched, tan and wrinkled, lifeless as a raisin, a strip of dried fruit. San Francisco, the village, is wet, pungent, and moldy, dripping and soaking from a fog that never lifts, eternally gray and then stinking from moist and mildew. Wetness abounds while just 400 miles south, dry as a bone, the desert that is Los Angeles yearns for water, wants where there's none, a thirst and a direness that crawls on all fours, parched in a struggle for survival.

And San Francisco goes, "La la, la la, la la," splashing and stomping and spritzing but smelling so bad. The outside walls of the Victorian buildings are wet, the corners of the windows moist from the inside, the welcome mat on the doorstep heavy with dank, the awnings overhead forever dripping, the curbs and the streets dark from the soak, the tracks of the train and the manhole covers and grates to the sewers are beaded, slick and slippery. Nothing ever dries there and in the sog and the wet, the fungi thrive, the spores spread, fruiting bodies burst forward, and magic abounds.

The magic had been there, it already existed, left over from the forefathers. The hippies had been at it long before we arrived, their remnants were everywhere. Patchouli and incense still hung, colors of the Victorians mismatched and wild, stray dogs on the streets roamed rabid going, "Where did they go?" The theatrical fervor and witchery of the hippies came from within, growing from a source of a need to share, a show-off of a soul that ached to give and to thrive, to make and create. Making things. Homespun crafting, bold musical expression, collaborations of personality and banter, a potpourri of mediums, speech and humor, wit and desire, but hand-executed with tools, physical dawnings of the spirit. Like markings in a cave, these gestures would exist forever. Without the pieces, the work, the costume, the beads, the song, the tangible outcomes that resulted, the magic would have withered. There were artifacts, though, relics they had made that we could hold in our hands and examine. A record by a band called Moby Grape, a tie-dyed head wrap, a smoking pipe carved from a stone, a dream catcher. Waltzing in on the heels of their movement, we kicked their magic aside, stomped it away to make room for our own.

Hippies had thrived, they'd owned it and harnessed a medium, profound and original, paving a path not less traveled but a path that couldn't have even been imagined, something unfathomable. Theirs was a look and a lifestyle, rabid and remarkable, half-bred and tribal, that bucked so strongly against the rest of the world that it shattered the placeholders. It flowered so quickly, its roots broke the pot. And then came us. As if. Who were we? So determined. So confident, so brazen, so cheeky and flippant. We had the nerve, assumptive spirit, and fuckery to flip what they'd done before us upside down, on its head. Aching for a turn and a movement, we needed to be part as only children can be. The only option for us at that age was to make it our own.

We encountered the hippies first, living above them in a five-bedroom flat for six on 16th Street between Valencia and Guerrero. Joan found the listing in the back of the newspaper, she'd circled it in pen as we all crowded around. She called the number from the pay phone and the rest of us followed. We were so young and had no experience in renting or credit check or anything that it took to secure an apartment, but Joan had lived on her own, she'd done this before.

Six of us took over the third-floor flat that we called the Island of Human Kindness. That had been scrawled, not by us, in a pencil that never went away by the mail slot in the caged vestibule that opened out onto the street on the ground floor. The apartment sat above a health food store, a haven and hippie mainstay, a co-op called Rainbow Grocery. We barely knew what health food was at the time. They sold wheatgrass juice and organic produce. It was run by a collective of long-haired elders, quiet and ambitious, political with their heads down. We'd go into the store but not to shop. We were intrigued and persistent, doing intel. Inside the space of the health food store there were bins of dried things and tubs of wet. Mung beans and growths in pickled trays, the smells were outrageous. Almond butter and seaweeds, bok choy and mustard greens, vitamins and probiotics in categories by the dozens. We wanted none of it but found it all fascinating. We called the health food store the Privilege Store because the proud attitude of the hippies was that it was a privilege to shop there. The notion of having to bring your own bags to a store was insanity to us in 1982.

Directly across the street from the Privilege Store was the Compound. Housed in an abandoned firehouse, it wrapped around the corner of 16th Street onto Albion, and declared itself proudly the world's first punk rock shopping mall. Which was cheeky and ridiculous, punk rock being the antithesis to the very concept of shopping malls, the epitome of American consumerism, the institution we hated and banged against. The old fire station housed a record store, a used-clothing shop, a café, and a barber of sorts where kids from the East Bay and beyond came to get mohawks. The placement across from the health food store could not have been more poetic and we'd watch the conflict play out from our window on the third floor.

There was a constant throng of suburban young punks in front of the Compound in ripped denim and badges and Dr. Martens boots and straps. It was 1982 and the boldness and confident swagger of the punks was impressive, remarkable. Some lived with their parents, coming into the village for the weekend, and we judged them based on that, but again . . . it was 1982. Punk rock blared from inside the building onto the street where café tables were set up on the sidewalk. Outside, boys with shaved heads skanked and shouted at passersby and cars on the street while their mates crouched against the wall, sitting on the pavement in rips and overcoats, mohair sweaters and stocking caps, homemade tattoos and fishnets, costumed naively, figuring it out, smoking, shouting, arguing, laughing, all of them extras in the movie, vying for a part.

Across the street from the doorway of the health food store, the hippies took it in. The field was set for an absolute clash between the old hippies and the younger punks, but there was a surprising air of acceptance that came from both sides. The elders looked on, leaned against the outside of their store, folded their arms, and acknowledged the youth, recognizing their rebellion, while the punks in turn respected the hippies. Two separate tribes, assessing each other and establishing a common ground in rebellion. This was the village and the time: tolerance, radical tolerance and acceptance, unrequited but reciprocal props.

As young punks ourselves, to clock the world morphing and changing from the top floor of our Island of Human Kindness was unique and a privilege, an eavesdropping of a cultural shift. We'd watch from our window the village unfold; it was just getting started. The tableau played out in a capture of cultural narrative, a snapshot that we were a part of, a crisp cusp on the edge of history. Like the books my mother read, tales of real things with fictional colorful characters. The scene and the movement were changing in the moment through our huge windows, from the street seeping in and us seeping out. Worlds collided, heroes and conquerers, San Francisco in so many ways was itching and growing and making it work, carving out a place for a new generation that we were a part of.

Children at that age are cantankerous, suspicious, doubtful, resentful, questioning, presumptuous, pointing our fingers at others first and then each other, asking questions later. Dozens of notions of foul play and mistakes and incorrectness abound, it's what we did, it's what we still do. Through it all the cream rises, the coldness sinks, we find each other, and a collective results. There we were, though, initially, united and bold, ready to fight. So quick and so young, so astute and obnoxious, the accidents we stumbled into were the ones that stuck. My tribe found me and I found my tribe. At that age, and in that age, the things that drew us together were glaringly simple. A bare ankle in an old man's dress shoe, an old-lady purse on a young person's arm, a boy in a trench coat with a button dangling from a thread. These things, these looks, these adoptions of nostalgia and age weren't ours, but we'd reinvented them out of thin air. No one told us to dress that way, we reached and sorted through the closet of what had been and made things our own. A badge on a jacket, a hole in a sweater across from you on the bus, a boot on a girl, a rip in a stocking, these details all clues that you and I could get along, could talk, could share, could fuck or be friends.

The notion of family shifted and redefined itself into what we were becoming. There were four of us that stuck. Billy. Will. Joan. Me. Billy and I had grown up together and moved to the village separately but together. We'd grown up wrecking authority, kicking convention, and challenging norms. Joan was a photographer who was already living on her own. She mothered us in a quiet way, selfless and uncomplaining, taken for granted in the way that mothers are. She chopped her hair bluntly, it hung in an asymmetrical flop, her boots weren't Dr. Martens but cooler than that, her trench coat a man's. She brought her camera everywhere. Her tactics and methods were focused and specific. The finesse and angle employed with her paintbrush on the trims of homes we painted years later. She'd taken to the job and the craft way more eloquently than I. Her face close to her work, squinting into the layer of paint as she coated the detailed surface flawlessly. The oil-based paint was tricky and less forgiving. Comparably my work was a wreck, I'd tried to smooth out the bumps and irregularities of my strokes with my fingers like a child.

Will was a friend that Billy had made from Berkeley, a philosophy student, attentively withdrawn, naively astute, his papers for classes he'd write in longhand, meticulous capital letters, tiny and succinct on the paper, page after page of rant and intellectual speculation. Big eyes like an angel, a loose cardigan, fussing at a dirty stove with a moka pot, exotic and out of place in our barren kitchen.

Beer bottles and a spilled bong, dirty plates and forks, magazines and flyers and ashtrays everywhere, never furniture, only mattresses or futons in our individual bedrooms. Some had sheets, some simply sleeping bags, pillows uncased and stained. An eventual red kitchen table we bought at Thrift Town, two chairs and two milk crates we'd sit on, one bathroom we'd share, our toothbrushes mingled in a dirty mug on a sink next to a bar of soap that would move to the shower and back to the sink. A black oversized plastic bag sat full with our trash in the smelly alcove at the back of the apartment. A turntable and speakers in the fireplace of the living room and stacks and spreads of records, fanned out, covering the floor.

Our rent for the flat was $160 apiece. Burritos were two dollars. Eating half, we'd save the second half for tomorrow. Fold the aluminum foil around the stump of it and put it in the refrigerator. At night we'd drink cases of cheap Brown Derby beer that we carried home in boxes from the big supermarket. We'd steal meat when we could and cook big steaks in a cast-iron pan. The fire alarm would go off, we'd disconnect it and get drunk in the smoky haze and piece together the puzzles on the insides of the caps of the beer. The world and us in it was wobbly and hilarious, there wasn't a time when we weren't arguing or laughing. I was already good at getting drunk, I'd learned it as a child.

2

....

I n Los Angeles we had learned to drink and then to drive long before we were allowed to. As children, fourteen or fifteen years old, we'd listen alone, late at night in our beds on our backs, and wait for our homes to go still. When all in our houses had settled, we'd sneak, separately stealth and sure on our young feet, avoiding the creaks and the spots on our stairs and floors, and slip sideways and backward out of windows and doors, the latches and handles of which we'd coax gently open then closed like dependable friends. One by one we'd meet on a street corner that was close to us all, on a well-watered Hollywood lawn, whispering and spread-legged in our shorts, waiting for the others to show.

Taking turns, one of us would bring the keys to a family car and we'd go back to that car together. With one of us in the driver's seat, navigating in the rearview mirror, the door barely closed, the other five would push that big car silently, backward, in neutral, out of its driveway and onto the street, down some houses from where it had sat. Far enough where it was safe to start the engine without being heard. We'd all ease in, still so careful and quiet, opening and closing the clunky doors, and drive up into the Hollywood Hills with liquor we'd bought or stolen from the store that sold to us with no IDs.

Up in the hills, away and alone, we'd drink ourselves sick, gulping and swallowing a mix of concoctions in a mad rush to feel crazy and brave. Throwing up and screaming, wrestling and tackling each other, wasted and ridiculous in bushes and on dirt trails, arms linked over our shoulders, singing and stumbling, there was nothing ever we didn't or wouldn't do. Back in the cars we'd bully our way through the streets of Los Angeles, throwing bottles out the windows, music on as loud as it would go, distorting in the car speakers, harassing anyone, drunk at that age, driving recklessly without licenses.

Obliterated and sick and spent, we'd get out of the car down the street from our homes, turn the engine off, and push the car slowly and silently back into its spot, the driveway where it had been. Like thieves we'd cover our tracks, wipe the backseats of bottle caps and dead matches, and sneak back through the windows of our houses, hooking the car key back in its place and tiptoe past our sleeping parents up to our bedrooms.

We learned the locations from the older sisters who'd done this before us, driven drunk into the hills and discovered the places. Meet at the Field. We'll go to the Trail. After the Treehouse we'll climb the Sign. Climb the Sign.

From everywhere in our neighborhood we could see the Sign. It had been repaired and rebuilt after being a shamble of an icon for a lot of years. We saw pictures of it on the wall of a café at the bottom of the hills, one of the diners we stopped and ate and ran out of without paying. There was an older black-and-white photograph of it in a frame on the wall of the hallway that went from the tables of the diner to the bathroom, and the sign at that time read, *HOLLYWOODLAND*. It had something to do with real estate, someone had said. A sort of advertisement for selling property. In the seventies some marijuana activists extended the O and the O of HOLLYWOOD with long white sheets, making the sign read, HOLLY-WEED. My sisters and I saw that in the morning after hearing about it on the radio and ran out to the front yard where we could see the huge letters on the hill through a muted blanket of morning smog. I felt a kinship for whoever had done that. The mischief and liability of breaking rules in the dark.

By the time we climbed it, it had been rebuilt and made over, the letters were impossibly massive, herculean walls of thick, corrugated steel. There were ladders up the back of each of the letters. We'd park the car far below at the end of a two-way road that only had room for one direction and we'd carry bottles of beer up the steep trail in pockets and backpacks, falling and drinking, twisted and cronked, stopping and starting again and again. We'd choose our letters, each of us on a different one, climbing the ladders and drinking, looking down at the flatness and the sparkle of Hollywood below. It was magic, high up on those letters, above the city, on that sign so majestic, and us, five or six drunk teenagers, holding on to the rungs of our individual ladders, perched, stupid, and entitled.

Somehow entitled as teenagers feels acceptable. The oblivion is excusable, commendable even. If I had children, which I never ever will, I'd *want* them to feel entitled. The ridiculous and naive pride, the assumptive mindset, it suits children, they wear it so well. As we get older and question ourselves, the entitlement stops looking good, it loses its sheen and allure and that mindset goes away. Not only are we not deserving of things but we might not ever have things. Even working hard, we probably won't get things, and besides, what we do get, we'll most likely lose. For now, though, dumb and drunk and driving around in our parents' cars, yes.

The Field was below the sign, down under Mulholland Drive, close to where Roman Polanski molested that underage girl at a party. In Los Angeles the destinations between places are only drivable. Well, that's not true, the Field was walkable from the Trail and the Treehouse was walkable from the Field. It wasn't just nighttime that we'd be up in these spots, but at night it was easier to sneak around unnoticed. In the daytime on the Trail, overlooking Hollywood and the houses below us in the hills with their swimming pools, we'd squat and roll and wrestle in the hot dirt, getting drunk and smoking, scattered up and down the littered narrow path.

There was an afternoon when two of us stumbled down the Trail all the way to a yard below, far, really far. A house with a pool like a million others, because it was hot and we were drunk. The rest of us watched from above as the two tiny figures from so far up climbed the fence, stripped down to their underwear, and splashed into the pool. As we watched, the owners of the home drove up to the front of the house. The two were underwater, horsing around, showing off, and when they came up for air they mistook our yelling and shouting from up on the trail as encouragement. All we could do was watch and laugh. It took a minute before the woman of the house came out of the sliding patio door and screamed for her husband. He came out with a broom and a phone in his hand. We knew the police were on their way so we scrambled away, back up the Trail, and drove off drunk to somewhere else.

* * *

Before we started stealing our parents' cars, we'd ride after school on our bicycles to Gourmet Liquors on Beverly, just west of Normandie. We'd bring our school backpacks and we'd each steal or buy quarts of beer. They never checked IDs. Someone had said that malt liquor was stronger and we all tried that. We'd take the quarts to Van Ness Park and sit in a circle and get shit-faced drunk in a corner by a wall of ivy where the grass smelled like piss and no one would bother us. It was near the tree my visiting cousin had climbed up into and wouldn't come down from. She thought we hated her and we might have.

At first a quart of beer was enough. We'd play games, crash our bikes into each other and catamaran on our skateboards, but mostly we'd drink and talk shit, like we'd seen our parents do at their cocktail parties. There was a phase where we did it in Spanish. Then we'd brag to Dr. Murillo, our Spanish teacher, on the schoolyard, that we'd been practicing.

One by one we got kicked out of school. Like the Boy Scouts. We'd all joined at the same time, it was before we started doing drugs. The same five or six of us had joined Boy Scouts together. We ended up in different patrols but we were all in the same troop. Troop 10. We were stirring up shit and mayhem already. Mostly throwing things off the tops of buildings at cars, doing our best to force accidents. We'd work our way to the rooftop of the Friday-night meetings and be gone for hours.

"There's just five or six of you," the scout leader would say.

We'd heard that before, in grammar school from the nuns. Those exact words.

"There's just five or six of you."

The rest of the world, the class, the troop, they were better behaved than us. We were the five or six who proudly lowered the bar.

3

. . . .

There was the same number of us in San Francisco, five or six. We worked as a crew like grubby fingers interlocked. We were fueled by a rush of desire to keep up, to make a mark, to claim a place for ourselves in the changing landscape. The places we went in our heads and the things that we did were encouraged by the friends we met and the past that the village had been. Butting our heads against the hippies and what they'd done and made for themselves, that was our own antiestablishment stance. It didn't make a lot of sense and it wasn't really fair. It was disrespectful, honestly, but that's what we did. The hippies had invented that stance. Nobly. They'd created a community and a movement specific to where they'd been, where we were now. The Haight-Ashbury and the Summer of Love and all that, that's what came before us. The hippies had resonated and made an impact, they'd changed the world. At our age, though, we were looking for something of our own. It felt more real to criticize and complain, to point out holes and flaws, to champion ourselves. What they'd done before us we saw as a reason to get up and scream.

More Plastic Bags was a warehouse space, tucked enough away to not attract attention. There were kids like us and hippies much older. It was a massive building of brick, floor after floor of flashing lights and sound removed from the street through a huge crumbled archway. We'd wait in a line for our turn to get in and see people we knew and meet pockets and clutches of weirdos we hadn't. Filmmakers, fashion people, queers, strippers, painted faces, bearded men in habits, couples wrapped in chains, masks, exotic gowns, wigs, the mix of San Francisco was a circus, vibrant, deafening and spiritual unto itself. Drugs were everywhere, pot smoke, meth on mirrors, tabs of acid on tongues of fucked-up dancers swaying into each other, obliterated, twirling and moving in throngs on the different dance floors, overstuffed couches on the edges of it all with crashed-out young people in crumples of costumes.

We'd run up and down from floor to floor, dancing and drinking and screaming over the noise of the party. There was a huge bowl filled with goldfish on a window ledge in the staircase, more like a party decoration, not an aquarium. It was situated in an alcove, positioned in the shine of a colored light. We crowded around the bowl and one of us said, "Everyone eat a fish," and we did. We ate the goldfish. We put our hands in the bowl one by one and scooped out goldfish and ate them. Live little fish on our tongues and swallowing them. No one judged, hippies looked on surprised and complacently amused at what the kids would do. Us eating the goldfish was just one of so many scenarios going on in the space.

We rummaged through the coat room and put on other people's clothes and tromped up and down the different floors of the party, wearing big floppy trench coats not our own, chasing each other through the crowds. Someone would approach us, not territorial or angry, honestly just wanting to understand.

"Excuse me, that's . . . You're wearing my . . . Is that . . ."

"Maybe . . ." and we'd run off screaming and hitting each other, laughing.

We found a plastic disk of pills in a pocket of one of the coats we'd put on. It opened up like a Polly Pocket. Someone knew they were birth control pills. We swallowed them all, ate the pills, and laughed about what would happen. There was a ring of different color pills in the center of the disk that we figured were the strong ones and I took one of those, expecting more of whatever it was we were expecting. Those were maybe the placebos that were eaten on an off day, we knew nothing.

Someone said Timothy Leary was there.

We didn't really know who that was but he represented something that had come before us.

"Let's get him."

We looked for him and wouldn't stop, asking the different hippies, "Have you seen Timothy? We're looking for Timothy."

Stoned hippies watched on, appreciative and impressed by our look and our energy. There was honestly no judgment.

"They're looking for Timothy," entirely unfazed and bored, mildly entertained. "One of them's wearing my coat."

We couldn't find him and we wouldn't stop and were enthused, even angry at the situation.

What would we have done with Timothy Leary?

No one taught us things. We stumbled into places and situations and paid security deposits and first and last month rents, split monies, expenses, and acted how we assumed people were supposed to act. Some of us had done this before but I hadn't and I had to listen closely to figure out how things worked, making blunders at every juncture. I left the curtain on the outside of the tub when I showered and flooded the bathroom. It hadn't occurred to me, I hadn't known better.

In fives or sixes we took streetcars and buses but mostly walked loudly as a gang through the streets of San Francisco. We'd go till we couldn't go farther, stopping where Market Street hit the water. The Ferry Building that currently houses a high-end farmers market of curated stalls and fancy things. Back then it was abandoned and we found a way to get in, jimmying a door that went up to the roof, where we climbed on the huge *Port of San Francisco* sign that lit up and made designs on the water of the bay. We played on the sign and scrambled around and drank the alcohol from brown bags we'd had grown-ups buy for us.

Those we respected, the outliers and rebels, the more provocative, the better, we supported relentlessly. Everything we championed, tonally and structurally, was right up next to us, in our mix. We were fully capable of changing the world and we did. Our directions and goals as they played out deserve statues in parks. We heralded loudly in a cacophony of strength and powerful prowess. We flew the flag we'd quilted together and rallied proudly.

We went out to public shows in the streets by Survival Research Laboratories. SRL were the older kids, cooler and insanely subversive. There was no one like them, their work was unprecedented, there'd never been anything like it, ever. They'd collect dead animals from train tunnels in the city and animate them with robotics, run them around in mock battles via remote control. They made bombs and explosions and constructed big machinery that fought itself. Can you imagine? Mark Pauline was the leader and he'd lost some fingers from his work, his level of commitment on display, he'd lost part of his fucking hand from an explosion. The performances they'd stage underneath freeway overpasses or in abandoned warehouse spaces were hugely influential, they coerced a movement out of us. Hundreds of us would go to their presentations and be warned to stand back by their crew with megaphones. Pushed back physically by the older kids, all wearing utilitarian jumpsuits and shouting into walkie-talkies. Bowling balls catapulted through homemade cannons at massive distant targets. The fallout was legitimately dangerous. Shrapnel flew, people got hurt from their performances, and we applauded the risks and the damage and the injuries. Their commitment to their craft was noble and exceptional, a higher realm. These were the heroes we looked up to.

Shows in San Francisco were where we met others. Outside of the clubs, on the sidewalks mostly, spilling out onto the streets, hidden bottles, cigarettes, fuzzy sweaters and fingerless gloves, under overhangs in the wet nights. The constant goal was to get in for free or backstage, always aiming for places we weren't allowed. The IBeam had a long and narrow carpeted stairway up to its entrance and we'd wait outside on the sidewalk on Haight Street for someone we knew to come out and smoke. If the stamp on their hand was fresh and damp, we'd lick our own hand and press ours against theirs. If that didn't work we'd pull from a collection of colored markers we'd brought and duplicate that night's hand stamp under a streetlight.

We saw everyone. Siouxsie and the Banshees, both nights. The Buzzcocks, the Birthday Party, the Butthole Surfers, Scratch Acid, Blurt, the Fall. Beer in the club was kept in the poolroom, under the benches we'd sit on. We'd open the boxes and steal the bottles and drink the beer warm. We learned to bring a bottle opener with us to the club and we'd sit on the benches, sharing the stash with friends we would make.

All acquaintances were made on the streets and at shows, on the bus and at work. I worked at a movie theater in an alley off Polk Street. There were sex workers and junkies who cruised our alley and we all became friends. Susan, the manager of the theater, had moved from Ohio. She and her best friend Clara were in a band together. Paula, who I popped the popcorn with, was from Arkansas. She was a clogger and sang, played the guitar and had a loom in her apartment. She had just joined a band called Frightwig. They were five women who screamed and were unlike any other. Tegan, who ran the projector, had recently changed their name. They were going through gender reassignment but we didn't have the tools to assign a pronoun at that point and they remained a he for a long time. These became my people and my world exploded from the inside out.

Gloria was an older woman with red hair in a wheelchair. She had worked for over twenty-five years at the Strand, our sister theater. Sometimes she'd come to our theater and work the ticket booth. She'd talk about movies, older movies, the ones we showed and hadn't seen. There was nothing she didn't know. We'd spread out in front of her like a campfire. She told me a story of a man who was first in line to buy a ticket when the

Strand opened every Sunday for every matinee she'd ever worked. She would get to work and he would be first in line. Every Sunday for years. One day he wasn't there and as she was opening her till she saw him arrive in a taxicab looking crazy and upset. He stood there and cried on the sidewalk. Through the hole in the glass of her concession booth, she stuck out her arm and, waving, asked the people who'd lined up to buy tickets to move aside and let the man come to the front.

The Strand was on Market Street, the lower dirtier part, around the corner from the Greyhound station on 7th Street. It was a two-story movie palace where I'd work sometimes because it was owned by the same people who owned my theater. It was cheap, maybe two dollars to get in, and there were three or four different movies shown every day. You could smoke up in the balcony and men cruised and gave each other blow jobs in the dark. The theater knew its crowd. They'd leave the lights off upstairs on the second level for the cruising. I'd go up there on my breaks.

4

....

I didn't realize what a privilege it was to be gay until so much later. Anxious and unsure, like unwrapping a present in front of a crowd. My surprise being watched, my reaction being clocked, the gift, though mine, revealed to me and everyone in the room at the same time. The ways I connected as a child to my gay brethren were unorthodox, wild, and dangerous, proud and shameful at the same time. How to explain to a tourist? How to understand the time? How to navigate a world in the dark with no map and no direction?

After my father died, I was telling a therapist about my sexual escapades as a young boy.

He came at me with, "So for how many years were you molested?" and I sat in the chair across from him and considered his question.

"No . . ." I started.

"Were they all adults?" he continued.

"Yes, but . . ." and I started to explain the situation. How consensual it all was, not predatorial.

"Were there *ever* boys your age?" he asked.

Technically, he had a point. It was difficult to hear, but in a book in which laws are written and lines are drawn, he was absolutely right. I was a child, underaged, and my sexual partners were adults.

It didn't then and it still doesn't matter even a little bit. I'd do it all again in a heartbeat, the age difference was nothing to me. If I had children maybe I'd feel differently, but for myself, it was real and consensual and I was acting out and becoming the gay man that I would become. That's what we do, what I did as a boy. I had sex with older men in bushes. Shamefully at first, proudly later. Fuck off.

Confused and lonely and finding my way, all I wanted was to be molested by a priest. I became an altar boy and skirted around backstage at the church before the morning mass as slutty as I could, fixated on that one intention. I was in a dress and would reach down suggestively and touch my young cock through the front of it, trying to get the priest's attention. The scent of the incense, the snuffing-out of the candles, the ringing of the bells, and the passing of a chalice, sexy and theatrical. The priest was an older Irish man and oblivious. Father Murphy. Bald and an ogre, thick-thick glasses, and a mole on his cheek, not my type at all, but still. I'd read somewhere a testimonial of a boy in Australia who had seduced his neighborhood priest. I'd assumed all priests in their chastity were fair game. It was all I wanted.

I was looking for cracks in the church's foundation as well, broken loopholes I could pry my young fingers into. I blamed myself when I didn't get the sexual attention I wanted. Glum and alone in that stupid colorless dress of the cloth, I was looking for guidance and direction, a road sign or course. That particular trail had not been charted on any map, the journey I'd choose I would need to find.

I'd noticed men in the bushes when we rode our bikes up into the Hollywood Hills as kids; I was twelve or thirteen. I don't know how else I would have known about it. I had no gay friends, there was no one I could talk to. As a gay boy, you notice things. Even at that age you know what they are. I don't know if a straight person could clock men, alone, coming in and out of bushes and trails, and know what that meant, but I knew what it was right away and I rode back there by myself as soon as I could. I'd notice later as I got good at it, when straight people stumbled on to the cruising scene, how long it took them to realize the game. There was confusion and an inability to comprehend. For myself it was quick.

There were men washing their cars in a big turnaround above a pond where we'd found the dead man. By then we'd started smoking pot constantly. We had weed and lots of ways to smoke it. Through a pipe, through a hollowed-out apple, through a toilet paper roll, once through a toothpaste box I'd got in my stocking for Christmas. We rode up into the hills and dumped our bikes in a tangle and fell into the grass by the pond. We'd been there before.

The park was at the base of the Hollywood Hills; you could call it the foothills but it wasn't really that. There was a small ranger station on the road that gave out maps to cars. It was at the top of a long incline so we'd ridden up that rise to get to the pond and were out of breath. We told ourselves we were at a higher altitude, and such being, we'd get stoned easier. We settled into being high, and as I leaned back on my elbows on the grass, I looked at the pond and saw, close to where we were sitting, the tips of the fingers of a human hand coming out of the water. Farther down away from the hands was the gentle profile of a nose, a chin, and farther down still was the top of a bend of a knee and then a shoe, the toe of a shoe. A dead person facing up. We all looked and didn't move. We didn't speak and we didn't move. We'd never seen dead before and we were stoned. Behind the body was a sign that read, No Swimming or Wading. It was both funny and not at all.

I hid our pipe in a bush, it was still hot in my hand. To myself and myself only, I asked who loved this man, was he dirty, did he have sisters, did he pray on his knees, and where was his mother? Still and quiet, cross-legged in a circle on the grass, we sat respectfully stern and un-sure, watching each other's faces, reading each other's reactions, taking slow stock. An older couple, he with a walking stick and she on his arm, slowed in their walk. Her body jolted when she saw what we had and the man steadied her.

"Oh for . . ." She turned her head away from it but kept looking with her eyes as the man shook his head no, no, no.

A younger couple, jogging, slowed; the woman stopped, her chest heaving still, her whole body breathing. The man continued to jog in place, then he stopped and put his arm around her. He pulled her shoulder close to his chest, said something to her face, and ran off, looking over there, here, around for help.

A silent ambulance arrived and a truckload of police. There were dogs and uniforms and nets and a man in scuba gear. The body was fished out slowly, ceremoni-ously. We stayed and watched from our spot on the grass. It seems like they should have eased the teenagers out of that situation. We were only thirteen or fourteen. We shouldn't have been there, watching that.

Above that pond was where the men washed their cars. It was a scene, the men and their cars, I'd seen them before we spotted the drowned man. Maybe they were polishing or doing detail, making things shiny. I took my bike up there later and rode among them. Through all of Hollywood and up into the hills. And being drunk, mostly. I don't remember having a bike lock, there were no such things as helmets. I'd take my bike with me. It was clear that the car detailing wasn't the spot, but there were trails and entrances to trails surrounding the parking area and other adjacents. Being a gay kid, it was simple to figure out.

There were entry points and paths that stretched into the hills in lots of different directions. Deeper into the park the trails got thicker, harder to get through. Bushed over, tangles of shrub. The more difficult it was to get through, the better. I know this clearly now, annexing ourselves away into the estranged and remotest parts of geographics is what we do as gay people.

Way, way down at the end, on the other side of where the nude beach is, past that, that's where you'll find the gays. Far out, beyond downtown and past the neighborhoods that are abandoned, kicked-in, and forgotten, that's where we build our communities. There's a history of the rest of the world wanting us away from them, and it works out 'cause we've always wanted to be away from the rest of the world.

The dirty narrow trails in the hills would get tangled and tricky to navigate but eventually spanned out into small sheltered alcoves. Men would hang on the perimeters and smoke. On the dirt were used condoms and old hairpieces, stained underwear, magazines, cigarettes, soda cans, bottles, a diaper. The diary of the ground was of the people who colonized there.

The crux of the park where all the trails met was like a high-roofed cathedral, hot light and brightness fractaling through a ceiling of branches like broken stained glass. In the speckled shine and illuminated dust we fucked freely, proudly, heroically, silently sharing ourselves in a fraternal flocking of cache and sway.

Our individual breaths were short and our fingers trembled on belts and zippers and complicated button flys. Rabid and feral and rushed, we drew each other close in twos and threes and circle groups of more. Men on their knees and down on all fours, pants around ankles, spread dirty asses slapped and fucked, cocks in our mouths and cocks being stroked with fists that we'd spit in and swat away the flies with. Tongues out, drool spilling onto the dirt, eyes rolled back, choking on irregular breaths, the rhythm of friction and propulsion beat quicker and louder into spouts of ebbs and flows.

The smell of the air, rancid and sharp, impossibly tangy, the taints and the breath and the sweat and the semen, condensed and then, as if spritzed like a fine mist of piss, falling and mingling with the dust in the air of the musky troposphere. All of us strangers, dancing and speaking in tongues in that wide-open fold with our same secrets.

It was magic being outside with the men, but a lot of the cruising in my youth took place indoors, in public bathrooms. The opportunity to stand at the urinal with other men on either side of you was unique and remarkable. Standing side by side, next to another man, our pants unzipped and our cocks in our hands. The dance of invitation as we stand still and wait. The charade and affectation of keeping your head still and moving your eyes to look down to the side without being clocked. The smell of the urinal cake and the roaring sound of a flush. The apprehensive, taut second of not knowing, before realizing that the game is on.

Working the urinal like a hungry little monkey, I remember seeing the phenomenon in the public bathrooms as a child and looking forward to it. My father never taught me how to use the urinal but I remember being so little that I had to get up on my tiptoes and rest my balls on the lip of the porcelain. I wanted it, whatever it was, it was a display case, a serving tray, a share space, and a mystery. A man standing next to me chuckled. Not in a gay way. Urinals were the beginning of a camaraderie and a pageantry. It was an initiation phase.

There was a department store near the Tar Pits that was a palace, a majestic deco building, the details not lost on me. A bathroom on the sixth floor. I'd started to seek out bathrooms when I was out. I'd been shopping with my mother and discovered that one. The men were older than me. More often than not it wasn't sexy, there were lots of very old men. I stood at a urinal and pissed on a man's hand as he reached over. He smelled his hand and I halfway pretended I didn't notice. Behavior and codes of reactions would span the map of acceptable and not. The type of man who would cruise a bathroom in a department store was different than the type who'd be outdoors up in the hills. The smell was glorious. Like piss and disinfectants. Both. That was the smell of sex to me as a child, the combination of excrement and cleaning it up.

Ideally there were two doors coming into the bathrooms so you'd hear the first door open and be able to compose yourself before someone would come through the second. Sucking or jerking off could stop quickly and we could be straight men, standing next to each other, peeing regular at the urinals. Like that, a light switch that instantly took the place of possibilities to a place of not, turned it back into a bathroom, straight and simple. All of our gestures were suggestive and covert, a language, second nature, hiding what we were doing, pretending to be who we weren't.

We'd go into the stalls. I'd go in and sit and wait. There was a code of tapping your foot or moving it slowly toward the foot of a stranger in the next stall. Without knowing anything other than his shoe.

There was graffiti, sometimes phone numbers on the stall walls that I'd memorize and call later at home in my young curiosity. Lots of times glory holes were hollowed out in the dividing walls. Sometimes they'd be covered up by sheets of metal and screws that went into the walls of the partitions. The genius of the glory hole. It can only have been created by a man. Something to stick a cock into. The nature of the act and the leap of trust is insanity. The notion of putting your hard cock through a hole and not knowing is desperate and reckless, a shucking and heroic act of defiance. The unspoken wild card is that someone on the other side could just as easily cut it off.

I don't know how I found the cruising spots but I know now that's what we do as gay boys. Aspirations lurked and propelled me to be a person, to carry the weight of defiance, to challenge a spectrum, to quench a desire. Young and separatist and alone and hungry, these are the times of a life.

There was a bar near my family's house below Paramount Studios called Griffs. I was in the back of the family car driving by on a Sunday and their function was spilling out into the parking lot. The lot was surrounded by a chain-link fence that was covered up mostly with black plastic tarp, though I could see through the gaps. We'd stopped at the long red light that turns onto Melrose. There were men in leather, harnesses, jockstraps, caps, chains. I'd never seen that and it scared me. I went home and got on a bike and rode back there immediately. Griffs was the epicenter of what I was looking for. It became habit for me to split off from the five or six of us after getting drunk in the afternoon and ride up to Griffs, cruising the neighborhood on my bicycle. I was fourteen.

The first man I met was washing his car in his driveway in a Speedo. He was saggy and tan and wore thick glasses; his eyes were small and friendly behind the thick glass, squinting and curious like a mole. I positioned myself in a way on my bike that he could see up my shorts. A foot on a pedal up high and a foot on the curb, young legs spread. Out on the sidewalk with the hose running, he started listing off the home improvements he was making. We talked and he asked if I'd like to come in and see. As we toured his home he brushed against my hard-on with the back of his hand, touching me through my bathing suit.

"That's frustrating," he said, "isn't it?"

I kept my responses to an economical minimum, shaking, excited, and scared.

"May I . . ." he said as he fumbled with the Velcro on my bathing suit. It was an OP bathing suit. He took me in his mouth and I came really fast.

"Okay, John," he said from his knees. I'd told him my name was John. As I rode my bike home, still drunk, I promised myself I'd never do it again. I got home and jerked off, trying to make myself think of vagina. My head went back to his mouth and the smell of his sweat and sawdust and I came again.

I'd go back and back to that neighborhood. It wasn't, but in my head it was what I was looking for. I'd go mostly drunk on the bicycle and ride around. It was close enough to my family home and I knew friends and acquaintances who lived around there.

Someone said once, "I see you riding your bike around."

What I must have looked like at that age, drunk and searching for sex. What does a hungry young boy look like? There were certain apartment complexes I'd gravitate toward. Manicured courtyards, Spanish interiors, scalloped tiles on stuccoed roofs. Regulars I'd collected after a while.

The man in the Speedo and I had a falling out, I'd likened the drama to a lovers' spat. I'd gone back to his house a couple of times, but at one point I parked my bicycle in his driveway while working another trick somewhere close in the neighborhood. The next time I met him he was cold and aggressively annoyed and told me he had syphilis. I'd never heard that word but I knew he was lying. In my head he was jealous that I'd left my bike in his driveway and found another man, but really I never understood.

I'd not talk as much as I could and never ask for what I wanted. I can remember the situations, the faces, the rooms, but I can't remember the act. I certainly wasn't good at what was going on. I had no references. There was no one I could talk to about anything. No pornography, barely pictures I'd seen in the magazines I'd stolen. I could only go with what I felt as a stupid and immature child. I wanted to press my body against a man's and gyrate really fast. To be held strongly and rubbed against roughly. That's what excited youth is. Bold and entitled. I didn't have to grow into that as a man. I was there from the start.

I got fucked but rarely. When I tried it, it wasn't working. I was too young. One night I rode up to the bar on my bicycle and got into a van with two leather men. One tried to fuck me and the other whispered, "Too tight." Getting fucked wasn't yet a turn-on, it just hurt. What happened, I wanted over quickly. I'd cum and get out of there as fast as I could, the fewer words spoken the better.

I told a man, a regular, not to say anything if I saw him out. That was important. The nightmare would have been me with the five or six of us at the ice-cream store, stoned in the bucket seats against the wall, and one of my tricks coming in and recognizing me. I hadn't realized the extent of the shame of us as gay people at that point. I was scared mostly that I'd be called out and discovered at the ice-cream shop.

We were all stoned and drunk in those seats of the ice-cream shop one night when my father came in. Out of place, wearing shorts with no socks, his legs pale and a big brown mole on one of his thighs. I was embarrassed.

"Now I've made some phone calls," he laid out. He was a lawyer. "You," pointing at one of us, "are staying at my house, you . . ." pointing at me, "are staying at his, you," another, "are staying at his house, and you," another, "are staying at his. So what is it?"

We looked at our ice creams. I would eat a mint brownie fudge sundae, I don't know where I got the money to buy that. We ended up all going to my house, all of us on our bicycles, and setting up the family tent in the backyard. We dragged the tent up from the basement and set it up together. After the lights of the houses had gone dark, we climbed the neighbors' fence across the street and slipped into their pool quietly. No splashing, no words, never caught.

5

····

Hiding things had always been important. I grew up doing it. Hiding who I was, what I did, the drugs I took, the men I fucked. I became an expert at lying and keeping things from people. I'd learned to carry books with a straight arm down at my side, not held up to my chest. Fingernails I'd learned to showcase with a closed fist rather than fingers laid out like a lady. It was hard, I'd grown up with three sisters and my mother and I had a special relationship. Do you remember the first time you heard a recording of your voice? For gay boys, this exercise is a nightmare. We are never aware of how gay we sound until we hear it played back to us. And then we try to fix it, to lower our voices, to present more butch.

It should have been easier for me to be open and honest about being gay in San Francisco when I got there, but it was complicated. It was a time for exploring and for establishing identities and creating art and personas. Our community honestly did not give a shit. About anything. The things that did register with people—flavors, eccentricities, character bumps—these earned credibility, not judgments. The actual attributes weren't as important as it was to be open about them, and proud of them. Alas. From where I was sitting I wasn't prepared to do that. I wasn't able to be open and proud. The hiding, the concealing, the inability to be myself came from a history of shame and guilt and suppression. It was deep-rooted and ingrained and a part of who I was. Hiding things and keeping secrets feels natural to most gay kids. We're raised to do that and we do it well. When the time comes that this is no longer necessary, it's a real pivot away from something not real to something real, and there's fallout. It took me a long time to get there. And besides, where would my art be without fear and shame?

I want to say that being gay was too easy in San Francisco, but that's only part of it. It just felt predictable. That was the thing. Which is ridiculous, but at the time I was fighting convention so hard. I'd grown up in Los Angeles where it was common, encouraged even, to be like everybody else. There was a cookie-cutter, cloned look and a persona that people in Los Angeles aimed for. It wasn't a place of originality, it was a place of uniformity and earning sameness among a bunch of normals. I'd fought that as a child to the point of leaving. I'd rather be anyone else than someone like everybody else. A category or demographic, even one on the fringe, felt cheap. It's still real hard to figure out who I was trying to be, but I was absolutely certain I didn't want to be like anyone else.

I was gay by myself in San Francisco for a long time. I found places and people and it was really different from my community of music and artists. Which doesn't seem accurate or even feasible, but that's the way I dealt with it. There were two different worlds for me.

In one world there was a bathroom on the third floor in the library at school. There were so many cruising areas in the park. There was the Castro. I hated the rainbow but it was another gateway into the village. San Francisco

morphed and opened and closed and presented opportunities and took them away constantly. Open windows,
closed windows, fast tracks and slow. Going out in the
morning meant staying out till night. There were people
I'd meet and things I'd bump into that would change my
day and take it in unimaginable directions. I'd go to the
YMCA in the morning and end up drinking absinthe on
a curb in North Beach, chipping a tooth, buying bad acid.
Taking a bus, meeting a butcher, flying a kite we found
in a trash can from the top of a hill that took forever
to climb. Plans were abandoned and nothing got done.
I never finished college and commitments were arbitrary
and seldom followed through. I made forever connections
with hundreds of people who I still call my friends. The
ones not dead, they're still in my life.

To have never acquired HIV. I think it's because I didn't
really have anal sex. Anal sex was the most common way
to acquire the virus. It hurt when I'd tried it and unless
a man was really pushy about it, I wouldn't go there. I
was promiscuous and had sex with strangers. Bathrooms,
parks, the YMCA. As I was coming out and coming to
terms with being gay, the fathers of my generation started
to die. Men left as I entered. I was part of it and not. I felt
it and didn't. The world was changing and I tried to not
be part. I'd seen the lesions on men's faces on the bus and
in the streets. It was easier to distance myself from the
plague than it was to accept it. Until friends started to die.
And I was sure I was dying too.

A darkness and a shroud, a panic in a street that was
subdued by design. A fog and blackness over a need to
scream, and then the hand that muffles it. With the hand
covering the face of a generation, the eyes filled with a

horror unseen, unprecedented, unimaginable. Looking first one way and then another, tearing up in a frenzy of terror, the face being shut out and shut down and silenced and somehow, in some general way, accepting the suffocating hand on the mouth as a given. To recognize that hand as something authoritative and regular, a presence and a regulatory suffocation that had always been? At first that hand was a given. The loss of lives, the mass genocide, the killing of a generation and community on the constant but temporary brink of a miracle, that hand was the devil. San Francisco learned to bite that hand, to snap a finger in two, the face of a people covered in blood from a hand that sought to cover up the death rattle, the howl.

There is a connection, a through line, there always is. I was convinced at every cough, every tickle in my throat, any visible abrasion, convinced for years that I had acquired the virus. More consistently life-threatening than today's version and so much more cruel in its targeting. Going to sleep and treasuredly fingering a sore on my leg. There would be so much to tell from the hospital bed. It would be the ultimate reveal, the unmasking of who I'd been and the definitive declaration that I'd be dead in months. Crippled with the thought of it, I didn't get tested again and wouldn't get tested. There's no better time to be aloof and irresponsible than as a scared and stupid child.

All my life there had been the encouragement to laugh at gay. It was a constant punch line. There were no role models in the periphery of any part of my life. The only gay men I was aware of on television were clowns, comedians, butts of a joke. Paul Lynde on *Bewitched* was Uncle Arthur, queenie and criticized, ultimately repulsive and a pompous windbag. I learned to adopt the homophobia it took to also be repulsed, and then that was that. With no positive examples in my life, I was alone and ashamed in the world I grew up in. I learned to diligently detest who I was. While San Francisco offered the opportunity to bury those lies and come clean, it was also too predictable of a direction for a compulsively provocative young man like myself to take. I wasn't exactly looking for acceptance. That came later.

6

....

In the Island of Human Kindness, as a group, as a crew, as a family, as a brood, we leaned into our shared common bond of music. It was easier to hide being gay when the focus of our young lives became the music. We had been going to the same shows, sharing our records, and bringing what we learned individually back to the group. We somehow as a group acquired a four-track cassette recorder and then a drum machine. I bought a keyboard and someone had a guitar. We started to work out compositions, something I'd never done, and the four-track became our lifeline. Taking turns and creating something from nothing. The notion of overlapping sounds on sounds became a credo. Sitting on the dusty floorboards of the common room in our apartment, in our baggy sweaters, huddled and passing around the only pair of headphones, we'd play things on top of other things, each of us adding our individual part to the music that evolved.

It was a sudden and profound plethora of opportunity. Knobs that panned to the right and the left, effects that altered sounds, different reverbs we could channel our instruments through, cords and extension cords and pedals and strings and outputs and inputs for days and days.

We were suddenly all musicians. I remember finding a guitar pick in my pocket as I dug for change at the bus stop and that surprised me. The same way I'd find a lighter in my pocket a long time after I'd started smoking. I'd changed and hadn't clocked it.

How does the morphing start? I hadn't known what a cord was, how it plugged into an instrument or an amplifier. I didn't know what an amplifier was or what standby meant. It told me what it was. It was an amplifier. That's how it worked, it amplified. The world was so basic and literal in matters of the tactile. How easy it was to be someone new. To learn a new language, to find new brethren, to cultivate a new perspective. Making decisions and breaking through barriers came so naturally to us.

The music and the sounds that we collected were the only things we took seriously. We would pass around the records and lie on our backs in the cold apartment looking at the artwork on the covers and listening to the songs. Risks we'd taken at the record store, risks we couldn't afford, most always paid off. We'd buy records and bring them home and they became parts of our lives. We had good intuition for finding what we wanted, there was no way of auditioning what we were signing up for. How was it always at our fingertips? All that we wanted just fell in our laps. We appreciated it all. We really did.

Billy and Will went to school in Berkeley, Joan and I both went to San Francisco State. Billy had met a drummer at school, an English major named Mike who was wound super tight and loved words. He didn't stop talking, hyperbole, ever. He was ruthlessly enthusiastic. My sisters called him the Elf because he worked in a bakery and later at a toy store. The two of them, Billy and Mike, started a band together. The singer, also named Mike, was older, maybe in his early twenties. He was serious, with an agenda, very serious. A man named Wade, who I eventually replaced, played the keyboards. The band was called Faith. No Man. With periods.

We all supported their band. We were devoted to holding up our own and championing our people. We would all put up flyers for their shows with staple guns and masking tape on telephone poles, on bulletin boards, near the doors of cafés. We told our other friends about the band and went to the shows enthusiastically. There was a tone shift in the village and we were part of it. Punk rock had happened and collided intensely with the hippies, but a new movement was taking hold. It was a darker sound, heavy, slower, rhythmic, tones of death, decay, disparity. It looked it. There were mostly black clothes, some white face paint, you could call it goth, looking back on it, but we didn't consider it that. Swaddles and textiles of the street, we spawned from what the city was. There was rain, there was gray, there was angst and anger toward the random responsibility of fronting a generation, there was art school, there was graffiti and things that combusted magically from out of nowhere.

Faith. No Man. took leads mostly from English bands like Joy Division and Killing Joke. The pummel and feel of that band particularly. Mike, the drummer, was listening to African rhythms, studying specifically that at Berkeley. From there the door opened to Jamaican dub. That became a sound that we'd listen to as a household. As we continued making music in the house, we tried to replicate the sounds we were hearing. Billy bought an Echoplex, a tape delay machine, from somewhere, the analog echo was everything. It opened up the world of sound-

scape and atmosphere to us. I had an ear for short me-
lodic statements that started as spouts of sarcasm in that
dark musical realm but always rang clear and stuck in my
head when I walked away. Buoyant and optimistic did
not belong, and I embraced that dichotomy. Forcing what
didn't belong. Accentuating the loudness of the presentation of song in a world that wanted to be intense. It was
always like an inside joke. I could let laughs happen, but
inherently, intensely, I clung to the presentation of melody,
citing it as my own.

As we grew into the village looking for ourselves, our
journey became less about making friends and being liked
and more about provoking the world around us, carving
new things into old walls that didn't belong. We followed
the trajectory of exploring what wasn't cool and what
wasn't allowed. That was a big part of the shift that was
happening around us. The older kids had been so strict
with their credos and tastes. So much was just not permit-
ted. Theirs was a rigid protocol with regards to what was
accepted and not. Obvious rules we'd adhered to in the
past. Post-punk was dark and the tones we employed as a
community reflected that. Black, always black. Bright colors were shunned. Brooding and introspective, yes, cheery
or hopeful, not, no. As we came into our own, we learned
that the offensive things attracted us most. A stance of
naive provocation became our go-to.

We put our money together as a household to get a
cable box and MTV. Only because it was so wrong. MTV
was the enemy. The gatekeepers of the San Francisco we
lived in would never. The small pools of elders, artists,
intellectually elite, older kids who were well read and
dressed cool, they looked down their noses at us as we

connected that cable. Their influences and references had dominated our world, but being next in line, we made it a point to shit in the pool we all swam in. I'm not being proud but I was then. Provocation was key and upsetting people felt important.

There was a band called the Sleepers that we respected in that way. They were the older kids and their legacy was honestly untouchable. Ricky Sleeper, the singer, had impossibly long black hair, it was his trademark. The sound was phenomenal but his hair was their legend. Long and straight down his back like a visionary dark angel. His craft was a grip on living in the village on heroin and suicidal ennui, the trope of being tortured and misunderstood that we all related to. At some point Ricky passed out on dope somewhere and the people he was with cut all his hair off. However it came to pass, we acquired a braid of the cut hair, it had been shared around the village after the incident. We dangled that braid from the rearview mirror of a friend's car. This was an example of kicking at the shins of the gatekeepers. We were disrespectful and antagonizing, not settling for an old guard. The toppling to us was gleeful and a triumph of our crusade.

A legend in the village we were drawn to was Ginger Coyote. She had been a football player in high school in Iowa and was part of the first wave of San Francisco subversive. She scared us at first and held our ultimate respect. I was young and impressionable and intimidated by what I hadn't yet experienced. Her hair was purple, her eyeliner dark, she was wrapped in rips and fishnets and her literal size was phenomenal. She was at every show and we became friends. Her bag was full of the fanzine she published called *Punk Globe*. It was an irreverent tak-

ing down of the system, a mash-up of local punk rock culture fused with television references, mostly soap operas.
This take on the system and twist on what was revered in
art circles we applauded and got on board with. Ginger
was a hero.

It wasn't enough to be different. The talk was important but the walk was everything. Writing music, making
clothes, creating photographs, paintings, making films. I
got accepted into the film program at San Francisco State
University. There were twenty of us in the program and
it had no pretense of being close to anything practical or
commercial in its leanings. Our work was deeply rooted
in art film. Brakhage, Makavejev, Kubelka, these were
our pioneers. Hollywood was far from what any of us
wanted, it didn't exist for us. It was of no use. We had
begun to see Tarkovsky and Warhol, we aimed to push the
envelope further and the notion of traditional narrative
meant nothing to us.

The first film I made was a short, in black-and-white,
of my friend Paula, a Trojan helmet on her head, wearing a weathered Victorian dress and army boots, moving
a dead duck on a chain from left to right. I shot it in
the stairwell of the Vats. The Vats was an old abandoned
beer factory near our apartment where musicians lived
and squatted. We stumbled into it at one point; friends
rehearsed there and set up studios. The film was meant
to explore the concept of the left side of the brain versus
the right. Movement in the film I'd directed in that way,
moving objects from the left to the right; syringes lined
up in a row, sculptures of old composers, the dead duck
on a chain. I don't know. What was it about animals?
My second film was *Pets*. A couple, Greg and Susan, are

on the phone trying to adopt a baby as we see their pets in the background in various forms of abuse. Honestly. What was I thinking and where was I going and where had I been?

7

....

My father was from Rapid City, South Dakota, and he'd had English bulldogs as a boy. I have a framed studio photograph of him at thirteen in a dapper suit with his dog on his lap. His hair is slicked back, handsome like a movie star, upright and eager, the dog coming out of focus and off his lap, its head too big, like a lion. We'd found the photo in a stack of things in a drawer we weren't supposed to be looking through when our parents were out of the house at a cocktail party. That dog's name he'd told us later was Bowser.

Instinctively, it was his fundamental goal to replicate his childhood for us. We all just wanted to fit in, us with the other screaming children in the neighborhood, he, too, fiercely keeping up with the other fathers, their cars and the ways in which they took stock and celebration with their manicured families at nine thirty mass. We all aimed for normalcy, acceptance, a passivity of foible we hadn't yet embraced. Part of the presentation and the idyllitz was the dog, the family dog.

We went to an English bulldog breeder, picked out a puppy, and named him Bowser. We drove him home, cradling him in the backseat, pampered, and passed him around as careful and fragile as a carton of eggs, set up a bed of blanket curled in a bun on the ground between the beds of our shared bedroom. Then he died right away, within days. Death was new to us, we'd seen *Little Women* and were familiar with Beth, dying of scarlet fever. Our tears and our mourning for dead Bowser were real but dramatically charged. We went back with our father and bought a second puppy immediately and named him Bowser. He died as well. We bought a third one after that, named him Bowser again, and he died. A veterinarian, years later when I'd bought a bulldog of my own as an adult, told me in his office, "Well, they're manufactured, they're not real, they're not meant to last."

The fourth bulldog we got was a girl and we named her Sarah. As puppies, these dogs are heaven, adorable beyond comprehension. Folds and wrinkles of fur, the poise and demeanor of an artisanal doll, Sarah was everything. Our father joined in as we pawed and coddled. It was exactly what he'd aimed for, moving west with my mother and starting a family, a yard, a fireplace, a car, a dog. It all fell so quickly apart.

Sarah was a monster. It started with chewing up cushion corners, tussling with a shoe she wouldn't let go of, destroying a purse, ripping apart a pillow, things our father assured us were normal. Until she turned on us. Sarah became something dangerous, a demon, something to be scared of. She'd see us coming out into the yard and charge us, go for our ankles, the pant leg, but biting through it and breaking skin. She was very strong, an unstoppable beast. We'd climb up on high things to escape her and call for the others to save us. It took three of us to walk her, one to distract her, one to grab her from behind, and one to leash and collar her. There were times when she'd be distracted enough to go on a walk, but usually she'd just attack us when we did. She became legend in our neighborhood, everyone knowing her name and shouting "Mad Dog!" at her in her rampages.

My father continued to forge a relationship with her but my sisters and I gave up. The only other person who engaged with her was Larry the milkman. There was a refrigerator in our garage and Larry would deliver the milk in glass bottles. He'd go through the driveway past Sarah to get there and he'd bring her a carton of cottage cheese that she'd shove her big face into, pushing the plastic container up and down the driveway. We'd hear it scraping the ground. For that favor, Sarah tolerated Larry. She loved cottage cheese.

It was a two-step process for us to get the milk from the refrigerator in the garage. It became second nature to grab a handful of dry kibble from a sack on a stool in the corner of the kitchen before going outside. To throw the handful over the fence before going through the gate and into the driveway to the refrigerator in the garage would guarantee Sarah's distraction for as long as it took. As fast as we could, we'd scramble through the fence, grab a bottle of milk, and get back through the gate before she'd finish with the kibble and charge us. Sometimes she'd forego the kibble, ignore it and go for our ankles, but mostly the diversion worked. When it didn't, one of us would get stuck out there getting the milk. When that happened we'd have to climb on top of the refrigerator and yell for someone to bring more kibble. It was normal for us and this became what a dog in the family meant.

We lived with Sarah this way for years. Tortured and attacked, contentious beyond explanation, we'd look enviously at other families and their dogs. We were living through a penance of a punishment. We weren't good enough to have earned a dog that would love us.

When we went away on a family trip, my parents paid John Petrovich to feed Sarah and keep an eye on the house. The whole neighborhood knew Sarah's legacy; he knew what he was signing up for with the job. My friends and I had started smoking weed and drinking by then and John Petrovich had a party at our house while we were gone, I found out later. The front gate had been left open and when we got home, Sarah was gone.

We weren't worried, Sarah would escape regularly. She'd get out and typically work her way up to the farmers market in Hollywood, far from our house, and find Larry the milkman, who'd bring her home in his truck. If that didn't happen, we'd call the SPCA after a day or two and they would inevitably have her. We'd pick her up and begin again. When she disappeared after that family trip, we went through the regular protocol to no avail. She wasn't around. Over a week passed and then more. The SPCA hadn't seen her, they knew her, they even knew her name, but they hadn't seen her.

After a couple weeks I was in the back-back of a station wagon miles and miles from our house coming home from baseball practice in a foreign neighborhood I didn't know with a carful of kids, and I saw her. Sarah, up on a lawn, getting busy on her own with something, sniffing around the underside of a hedge. Undeniably it was her. It was odd to see her so out of place, out in the wild, like a celebrity in a pedestrian setting. We slowed at a stop sign and I started to say something and then didn't. I turned my head and looked the other way. We never saw her again.

8
. . . .

We moved into a new apartment, Billy, Joan, Will, and I, and in an insane twist of fate, one that changed the course of my everything, the keyboardist of Billy's band quit and I stepped in. You join a band and the sky opens, there's nothing but optimism and opportunity, suddenly, to be in a band. To have a cause and a purpose, a way in which to walk, an identity formed suddenly by a different metric, things I'd only aimed for. Straight up. Everything changes.

Mike, the drummer, and Billy and I met and converged at the crux of the cohesion of our personalities, our chemistry. The three of us. We took on an agenda of culture and future and funneled the tactile of our everyday into what we aimed to be. We listened to more dub music and smoked more weed. We discovered the Last Poets, the Black American collective who preached Black radicalism. It was an insane appropriation on our part but we started to wear dashikis and grew our hair into dreadlocks. We'd never seen that before.

Dreadlocks became an obsession. Have you ever smelled a dreadlock? Held it and broke it open like a baguette in your hands? The smell is astounding. A diary of days and memories, specific and widespread, tangent and pungent, historical and remarkable. Growing our hair and letting it go wild in that way was a commitment and a gesture of strength and solidarity among ourselves.

Politically and culturally it wasn't something that was ours, and that's a testament to where we were, entitled and trampling a tableau that we had no excuse to be on. Mike, the drummer, had naturally curly hair and it started to dread up when he stopped washing it. Mine was straight and I damaged it with hair dyes and bleach, never washing it, twisting it into knots as it tangled. We were obliviously naive to the complicated nature of what we were doing. We had afforded ourselves the opportunity to take things culturally, that was a luxury of young children in that free zone. San Francisco looked on and did its best not to judge, though it's hard to ignore how grubby we were. There was respect and a sense of reverential awe, but there were absorptions and appropriations happening that were wrong and inappropriate.

We rehearsed in the Vats. There were long abandoned hallways and on either side were portals, window doors that opened up like the fronts of washing machines. There were round glass coverings and you could see into some of them. These were the vats where beer was stored, that's how we understood it. You would crawl through the windows into the long spaces. Inside those narrow rooms was where punks lived and made music. There was a puppet in one of the glass windows as we walked by that first time and a dish for change outside the door. I threw a quarter in and the puppet moved. Just a gesture. Twenty five cents' worth.

A lot of the peace-punk bands rehearsed there. MDC was one. They'd come to San Francisco from somewhere else. Millions of Dead Cops. They were political, they had an agenda too. We felt connected to bands that were stretching out in ways other than musical, even though our sounds were not so alike. We ended up rehearsing there at the Vats, sharing a space with another band. Sharing was how we made things work.

The peace punks were children of the hippies who grew up into their own versions of politically active. They'd been there all along. Some of their parents, the older hippies, were still that, older hippies. They just had different hair. They mixed with us and a lot of what happened came from a sense of family.

The peace punks liked our crew. There was a band called Trial who made flyers and fanzines based loosely on the graphics of Crass. They were relentlessly political and assured in their presentation. They worked with scissors and glue guns, putting together posters they'd staple up around the village. They were swaddled kids, activists in black clothes, drapey cloaks, Chinese slippers with homemade tattoos, visually stunning. One of them was growing dreadlocks like us, they had long hair, which in the face of new San Francisco punk was subversive. I played keyboards in a performance with Trial in the village's Civic Center for squatters' rights. The stage was set up in front of city hall and I brought my instrument and set it up on an ironing board—I didn't have a keyboard stand yet. We made noise and screamed for the squatters. It was the day I met Lynn Perko, she worked at a tiny diner next to the Civic Center and came to the protest. None of us would miss a protest. She was the drummer in the Dicks. She became a best friend. The family of musicians and activists covered most of the scope of the city; the areas we didn't cover we never really paid attention to.

We also rehearsed in the Tenderloin, across the street from the Sound of Music, where I'd play my first show with the band. We shared a rehearsal space with Frightwig there. The street scene was poisonous and alive. The drugs, the sex work, the chaos of us with our instruments, carrying things in and out. There was screaming constantly, the buzz of the brink of arguments, charged voices coming out of apartment windows, money changing hands, twos and threes of people walking quickly in clusters, syringes on the sidewalk, condoms in the gutters. There was a gate, a metal gate that let us into our building, where we rehearsed. The gate locked before the second door opened, a vestibule of a prison between the street and front door. Tile on the ground, newspapers, spent bottles in bags, cigarettes, I didn't mind getting stuck there in that space. We only had the one key and would have to wait for someone to enter or exit in order to get in or out. It was a parade of puppets and saints that flowed out onto Turk Street. I met a man in a bathrobe who leaned against the other side of the gate from the street. He pushed a finger through the latticed ironwork to where I was.

"You alright, little man? What's in that cage? Oh," he winked, "you're a musician."

The way he said *musician*. He wore a patchwork cap, a capital C hung from a chain around his neck, and a pager dangled from his terry-cloth belt. He was a pope and a prophet, there was a small bandage on his lip, tissues on his chin, dots of dried blood.

"Who shaved you?" I asked, respectful and sincere.

He looked away and smiled shyly. His name was Cotton. He helped us move our equipment later in his own way, clearing a path on the busy sidewalk, keeping an eye as we went back in for more of it. As young kids with in-struments, we became part of the fabric of the street.

In a natural effort to form an identity, Billy, Mike, and I made a distinct move to distance ourselves from the singer we'd been playing with. We'd made some head-way as a band with Faith. No Man. and we didn't want to lose the small audience we'd earned. We left the singer —I hesitate to say "kicked out" because he had techni-cally formed the band—but we decided to go out on our own as Faith No More. It felt empowering and rebellious. He hadn't understood our obsession with dub music and rhythms, incense and pot smoke. He'd been stiff and one-sided. The other three of us were embracing something, creating an ideology all our own. We were paying hom-age to old San Francisco but never intentionally. We were making fun of the hippies and throwing it in the face of the punks. Our cynicism wasn't lost, people got it.

In our daily lives, we approached our concepts and routines very conceptually. We intentionally removed our-selves from the traditions and conventions of other bands we knew. It was important to separate ourselves from the way other people did things. We started to strategize our shows as events, not just performances but happenings. We switched singers and wrote new songs for every show. Our goal was to hypnotize. The simplicity of the repeti-tion would transcend. It was real minimalist. I liked to brag about how I could type one hundred words a min-ute, I had the option to play like Liszt or Liberace on the keyboard but I was holding back in the execution, cre-ating something simpler, something with more discipline, something heavier. I was full of myself, determined and boastful.

Without a singer, just the three of us, me, Billy, and Mike, embraced our independence and formed a sort of ethic based around the weird lifestyle we were developing. We'd bang on things around each other, that seemed to be the start of it. Tabletops, kitchen utensils, pens and sticks, roofs of cars, anything near. We were obsessed with simple rhythms and we'd tap out loops among ourselves. That in its purest form was the start of the band we formed. Banging rhythms with each other. We'd be in our dashikis and dreadlocks anywhere. We loved the spot across the street from us called Café Pícaro. We called it Pick Your Nose. It was inhabited by the Rajneesh collective. They were a spiritual cult who draped themselves in only colors of the sunset, reds and oranges, and wore necklaces of wooden beads with their leader's picture. I was enamored with their look and imitated it, wearing swaddles of draping auburns. We made our own version of the necklace with a photo of Don Knotts around our necks. We'd bang our rhythms on the table of Pick Your Nose and drink bottomless-cup coffee and make flyers and brainstorm about the band. The band became all we did.

Taking the rhythmic loops to another level, we started to play our instruments in the same way. We'd make short loops, Billy and Mike on bass and drums, me on my keyboard, and play them over and over and over. The point was that it was enough. The simplicity and power of a minimalist loop was all we needed and it was heavier than anything else we could achieve. "Heavy" came up a lot. I was on board in the same way I got on board with God in AA years later. Like, your version of "heavy" and my version of "heavy" are clearly two different things but we can make this work. These loops were our toolhouse, our foundation, and what set us apart from our other musician friends. Our simple-minded attempt at monotony, minimalism, and repetition became who we were.

I got credit as it all played out, but my part in this mix was a spiritual glue. Without it, what the others were doing was barren. It was a heavy and unique pummel, spare and majestic. It was clearly a special base, created by special people, but it was just a foundation. Drum and bass by themselves were big and powerful but lonely and isolating. My layers of beauty or gay or pretty, whatever it was, on top made it what it became.

There was a premise to achieve these loops in an aim for a hypnotizing mindset. We'd light incense in our studio and smoke massive amounts of pot and take drugs we'd find. MDMA, acid, we'd go to places and spin out musically. We started to play with other people, one at a time, and that became part of the equation. The collaboration with other friends from the village.

We didn't have a singer and it felt like us as a collective was a more pertinent part of the project, the basis of what we were going after. Just the three of us and our loops. We didn't have a guitar player either. We recognized the importance of that instrument in our mix, but we were disciplined. We were really exploring what the three of us wanted to achieve and we were strict about it. Even socially, new friends kind of went through an interview process. We had an agenda and we needed it to be the forefront of what we were and what we did on the day-to-day, artistically. We continued our quest of these loops, the simplicity, the repetition, the discipline and focus of that.

9

....

Our first show as Faith No More was at the Mabu-
hay Gardens in North Beach, among the strippers,
the barkers, the beats, and the Italians. We had asked our
friend Joe Pie to sing. He was the singer of the Pop O
Pies, a band that did the song "Truckin'" by the Grateful
Dead over and over in different variations. It was high
concept for a punk rock kid to be doing that, ridiculous,
it made no sense. Our response and admiration of it was
excessive and real. Joe did mostly spoken word for us that
night and screamed, "Spirit, excellence, good stuff, further
down the road!" That was a line that stuck with us. The
music was like a mindful freight train. It did exactly what
we wrote it to do.

Onstage was a haze of incense and candles lit on
the tops of our amplifiers. Dashikis and dreadlocks. The
flames of the candles flickered close to the curtains and the
incense was thick and unbearable. The sound could only
be described as a pummel. A bare pounding of drums,
relentlessly repeating itself, like a skipping record. A bass
that moved in the same cycle, filling the space with a sway
and a motion and a groove. And on top of that, the bliss
and beauty of a high string section maybe, a choir, an un-
decipherable screaming of angels. None of it made sense
and then it did. We aimed to confuse. In that club, in that

year, among those people, we did not belong. We made it a point to not belong. There were some who watched us and got it and many of them honestly did not.

We weren't popular, we were odd. We were full of ourselves and irreverent and provocative. We were self-assured and pushing hard to make a point we weren't clear on. It felt good to work at something and then present it, regardless. The presentation was everything and that's what we did, we presented.

We continued to write music on the four-track cassette recorder in our apartment and we got better at it. We were generous with our equipment, we all shared what we had. Someone would record something and we'd add to it. The notion of layering things as a form of writing. The give and take, the push and pull, the adding and removing of musical parts to what we did became the whole, became who we were. None of us really sang, though. The music part, the instruments, the sound, was always coming first. The singer was secondary, inappropriately inconsequential, an afterthought. While the notion of the music was so high concept, the main voice or focal point of our performances didn't get a lot of creed or even credibility. We leaned into this nontraditional approach by accident initially, and eventually on purpose.

For our second performance, our second show, we played with a dashing and volatile vampire who I went to school with named Walter. He was alcoholic and intuitive, anxious and bold, sharp-witted, intelligent. He wore a trench coat and black dress shoes, his hair greased back into a sort of pompadour. His hands trembled. He was of that look of punk rock that threw back directly to the 1950s, a greasy-kid look, timeless, effortless, born that way. We had created new musical loops for the performance and gave Walter free reign, letting him do whatever he wanted. We didn't take much interest in the words or storytelling. It was more the consummation of all of our performance parts. Walter was drunk and reckless amid our sound storm. There was power and there was achievement. There was finesse and craft on every level.

From the inside out we slowly built a community. Glorious Din was a band that we played with. They were fans and there was a dark thread that connected us. Eric, the singer, from Sri Lanka, started a fanzine that I'd type for. Because I was fast, I could knock off the pages that were then copied at a printer and assembled and stapled together. I started to write for the fanzine, I'd listen to music as I typed and review it. Butthole Surfers, Swans, Einstürzende Neubauten—the fanzine was called *Wiring Department* and we were all part of it.

Another singer was Jim Pasque. He was a friend I'd met at film school. He was from Detroit and he made incredible work, short films of punch and rebellion. One was about a friend he tricked into getting into a cage and leaving him outdoors for days, filmed from the cameraman's perspective. Another was called *two shots* and slammed from a shot of a woman's face in the throes of masturbation into a second shot of a baby being born, jettisoning out of the vagina. He was a provocateur like us and relentlessly supportive of what we were doing. He stuck it out for a number of shows. His style was preacher-like. He'd rant mostly, not sing, and stalk back and forth on the stage evangelically. He lost a tooth somehow from a scuffle with a doorman after one of the shows and asked the dentist to sharpen his incisor teeth into fangs after fixing the missing tooth. He was a hero and a prophet.

Jim taught us games. One was Deprivation. You go around the room and list off things you've never done before, things you'd been deprived of. If no one else was deprived of the same thing you were, you got a point. I'd never seen *Star Trek*, for example. That always earned me points, 'cause everyone else inevitably had. I remember the game becoming a tool to find out things about each other. Mike Bordin once said in the game, "I've never shot up."

Another game was Trust. You worked in teams of two and took turns, one being the leader, one being the led. The led would close their eyes and not open them under any circumstance. Direction from your partner was given by time. "Twelve o'clock, straight ahead . . . Okay, one now, one o'clock, slowly, you're coming to a step . . ." Instructing the one with the eyes closed was the game, they'd trust you to take care of them directionally. The favorite part of Trust was when there was a space in which the leader could say, "Okay, now . . . run, you can run, you have all the room in the world . . . Run!" And being led, you could run fast with your eyes closed, with no obstructions. It was horrifying and exhilarating, a matter of Trust. Running with your eyes closed was a crazy privilege, one that required a real friend you trusted.

After two or three shows with Jim, we did another with Paula from my movie theater. She played saxophone and bass and guitar and she sang with a beautiful wail like a possessed witch, like an angry Emmylou Harris. She played guitar with us and screamed. I was comfortable and at home with a woman onstage. I was from a family of women, Mike and Billy weren't. Ours was more of a boys' club, the heavy part of what we were doing. I think the perspective and the tone of who musical men were on that map at that moment kept me in the closet longer than I needed to be.

10

·······

The village unfolded and spread its wings and I learned accordingly. It wasn't all safe and it wasn't all healthy. In the armpits of the city there were mites and I'd choose to settle in places I wasn't allowed and was scared of. In the nestles of dark and questionable and the realm of warnings and hot spots, I'd find overlooked and discarded things and make them my friends.

It's a talent I have. I still have it. I see the good. It's as simple as that. I gravitate toward the good in people, and if that good is shrouded in complications and surrounded by land mines, I'm intently more attracted. If it takes work to see the special in someone, I am more than game to put the work in. The outcome has always been potent and charged and unexpected with friends I've made who others have shunned. I talked about it at my father's funeral. I don't remember what I said exactly but I likened myself and my acceptance to the unwieldy as a trait he'd passed on.

My intuition with regard to friends has never been conventional or convenient. I'm attracted to boundary pushers, unorthodox thought, and outrageous trajectories. It's hurt me and helped me both. I've been burned and escalated, helped and hindered, I regret nothing.

We called her Laurie the Raisin because she wore

black clothes that were mostly wrinkled and she was a little bit rotund. She had a black spot on her iris that she got from an accident with a cactus as a child. It had happened on Christmas, the day before her birthday. When we met she was dating Eric the Goose. The Goose and the Raisin. She was a year below me in film school and we became inseparable. She was prickly and smart and took shit from no one. She lived in a neighborhood that smelled of mayonnaise. There was a factory nearby that churned it out and I could feel the mayonnaise in the air on my face as I'd ride my motorcycle to and from her apartment. It was wet in the air and it stung my skin.

We'd sleep in the same bed together and when we didn't we'd talk on the phone all night. We'd doze off and fall asleep on the phone together, our receivers in our hands, then wake up and talk more. What odd children we'd become. As the village spun round us I started to sleep in my clothes. I wanted to be ready, always prepared. Things would come up randomly and suddenly and I could jump out of bed at a second's notice. Eventually I slept with the lights on, it just made sense.

Laurie the Raisin taught me about Big Star and Alex Chilton, Václav Havel and Pasolini. She made a film about a girl on a bike getting scared by a snake. We stayed friends forever until she moved back to New Orleans and started a dog rescue after Hurricane Katrina called Used Dogs. She hanged herself in a basement when everything seemed to be going well.

Diana was the first of us to get attention, she was a porcelain nightmare. Stunning, like a statue, a Roman bust. Perfect skin and tangled hair from bleach and coloring, like mine, dreadlocked, unintentionally but inevitably gorgeous. A professional black-and-white photograph of her got used in a GAP ad and it was everywhere. On a bus stop in the Panhandle someone had drawn two round nostrils on her nose with a marker, turning her into a pig. To us this was success. Hers is the only vagina I ever tasted. I saw her last in New Orleans and she died shortly after. I never found out how.

Jim Olson was my first boyfriend. He was socially preposterous, a little bit older than the rest of us, confident and comfortable, like a saggy old dog. He knew more than anyone else, he had something to say about everything. He was a treasure of spirit, one of a kind. He'd school those of us who would listen in a ridiculous way; his theories and data bank of information, everything he knew, were outlandish and provocative. He encouraged disagreement and would argue with anyone, everyone. There was a small handful of us who could stand him. Most of our crew would avoid him and complain about him behind his back. He was fascinating to me. There was a spark and a liveliness to his eyes and his words that were threatening, captivating. I was engaged and enamored fully.

We didn't have a name for personality disorder. I'd simply clocked the condition as an eccentricity, a flair, an abundance of enthusiasm. A need for attention. A quirk. It turns out it's a sickness. I hadn't known. I was in love with a sickness, the flavor of it was new and dangerous and captivating to me as a young person. The extent of the danger wasn't clear; it had been intriguing firstly, then electrifying and ultimately deadly.

Our love had started with our feet as we laid next to each other in bed. We had been friends for a while and he knew I idolized him. His socked foot reached over and rubbed on the sole of mine. That first time we stayed in bed fucking for over three days.

Our sex was secret and incredible but I was smitten with his intellect. He taught me about the village and about living on the street. Gough Street was pronounced like "cough," not like "go." He knew everything there was to know about the cable cars, how they worked, the amount of impact and weight and friction they required. He took me to the cable car museum on Powell Street, ranting on and on. He shared a place he knew where it was safe to sleep under the Golden Gate Bridge and taught me how to make coffee outdoors with a Coleman stove. He took me on road trips in his Ford Mustang and showed me aqueducts we peed in that filtered the world's impurities. He schooled me on wilderness areas and we tracked mountain lions in the California desert. He was obsessed with Ronald Reagan and schemed of ways to assassinate him. All of his pontificating in his high-pitch banter you either turned away from or confronted head-on.

He taught me about the stock market. Of all things, the stock market. Kids with dreadlocks, living hand to mouth, doing drugs and making art, shoplifting, as subversive as we could be. In what world would the stock market interest children like that? What wild hair, what whim would encourage eccentricities like these? To my credit, I had a head of wild hairs but the extension of the flavors, the far reach of my tastes, the friends and the loves, the cast in my world, they changed my life completely. They flipped who I was from down to up and then back. I reaped the benefits of the decisions I made like a pawnbroker or a gambler with constant payoffs. My mix and the stew that I lived in were impulsive and pungent, bold and magic, never not delivering.

At the end as I muse, there is only hard proof and tangible, practical evidence that suggests my unorthodox approach to inviting sickness into my life was fruitful. The risks I took, dabbling with the challenging, the potentially problematic, they paid off. The times I had, the memories I chart, the money I made, quite bluntly. The flip side, though, there is one and I've never really cited it before now. I'm humbled in acknowledging the dark side of these friendships and now recognize that the consistent link or similarity that comes up in the relationships like these is the drugs. The drugs and the drugs and the drugs. The drugs and the drugs and the drugs and the drugs.

11
· · · · ·

Where did they come from and how did it start? I'd love to see a pile of them all just to get a handle. All the drugs in my life, a pile laid out on the floor. The heroin, the weed, the crystal meth, the bottles, the booze, the pills, the powders, the baggies, syringes, tinfoil, ceramic pipes . . . I want to see the pile, exposed, just as a starting point. Some drugs are for fun, there were together drugs, there were party drugs, there were exploratory get-to-know-your-friends drugs. Heroin was a drug to keep a secret. Initially as I dived into what drugs were and how I took them, I reveled in the hiding of it. It's what I did so well, I hid things.

I had a desk as a child, a huge wooden lawyer's desk. It was my dead grandfather's, I don't know how it got up the stairs but it was mine and took up a third of the entire space of my room. There was a lock in the drawer when it arrived. More than anything I wanted a safe place I could keep my secrets. Everything in my young world revolved around the things that I could hide.

I pried out the original lock in the desk with a big flat screwdriver I took from the toolbox we kept at the top of the basement stairs and rode my bike to the hardware store and picked out a new lock. I'd carefully measured the hole and bought one that would fit the desk. I had the only key. I installed it and made the face of the lock flush with the wood of the desk. Locked in the drawer was where my drug kit went. I organized it meticulously, rolling papers, a ceramic pipe, matches, a contraption I'd bought from the back of a magazine that rolled joints tightly. Next to it all was my diary, full of lies.

I kept the key to my desk on a ledge above the window I'd sneak out of at nights. I'd have to climb up on the edge of the foosball game to get to it. When I came home from school one afternoon, my father was sitting in the big office chair at the desk and my mother stood smugly beside him, her lower jaw skewed left in a sneer. I leaned in the doorway of my room and waited. It was a trap. My father started to speak. Breaking the trust. It was a phrase he'd used. It was my most popular infraction, the one I was constantly punished for. Breaking the trust.

"And here we are again," he was saying. "Back here. The trust, broken again, Roddy. If your grandfather knew what you were keeping in this desk, what you were using it for . . ." And he did the thing he used to do. He picked up an inconsequential something from the desk and put it down emphatically. The gesture of a lawyer. "I don't even know what to say."

And then a key appeared, like a magic trick. He held it in the hand he wasn't emphasizing with. It was the shape and color of the key I'd made and hidden, but the key he was holding was different. The head part of this key, not the part that goes into the lock, but the head part, was notched and irregular. The one I'd bought at the hardware store was perfectly round. I could see it was different right away. And then. He took the key, he put the key in the lock of the drawer, and I watched as it miraculously opened, slowly, dramatically, like the *ta-da* reveal of a meal under a dome. My weed, my pipe, my secrets, all in the open and laid bare. The impact of all of the things hidden revealed was like a breaking of a sound barrier. The space in the room actually crackled as the air touched my things, exposed in the opened drawer. My mother shined like she'd won a prize. She was making the face, her lips scrunched in and together, her expression just shy of smelling something bad, a hint of a smirk, sheer self-satisfaction. Not my father, it was different for him. He was deflated and sat back in the big chair, deflated and shrunken in his disappointment of me.

"If your grandfather . . ." he said again, and his voice just trailed off. His necktie was relaxed, his top button unbuttoned, he wasn't going back to work.

It took me a beat to get my bearings as I sat in it. Slowly and steadily, like Columbo, formulating my thoughts, in faux confusion, I knew exactly what I was doing. I lifted my head and held their gaze. "Where did you get that key?"

"I got the key when your grandfather died, and if he only knew—"

I lifted my hand dramatically, softly, silencing him, "Right. You said that." I paused, sure of myself and relishing the moment. Assuredly, confidently, I began: "I made that lock. I put that lock into the drawer. It is my lock that I bought at the hardware store. There's only one key to that lock and I have it." A beat and then, "So where did you get that key?"

My words landed like a heavy thud from an oversized mallet. My mother's face fell. No one spoke. I watched the triumph leave her body and I didn't move, I held my ground and didn't twitch. My father's disappointment was different. He fidgeted and looked at her quickly. She looked back at him, then both of them back at me.

"I don't know where I got that key," he came back with.

I let it hang there, the drama of the irony. In my head later, when I played the scene back, my final words were, ". . . the trust." For real, though, the conversation ended, my drugs were flushed down the toilet, and I found new places to hide my things.

12

......

We met Courtney through Deanne, who'd moved recently to San Francisco from Long Beach. Deanne was a punk rocker and was friends with 45 Grave. She was a hairdresser, she used to do water ballet and was getting into the Grateful Dead. That part bears repeating. She was a hairdresser, she used to do water ballet and was getting into the Grateful Dead. This was an unheard-of trajectory and it fascinated us as kids. She had her own car, also an anomaly, and hovered around initially like a comfortable cat. It was the first time I'd smelled patchouli. At first it's exotic, like a clove cigarette. Then it makes you sick.

Deanne brought Courtney to a show we played at the Fab Mab. Courtney came there fresh from Japan where she'd been stripping or hostessing or something. That part was never clear. She was wearing a wedding dress. That's how she entered my life, in a dirty rock club in a wedding dress.

She told me she would be our singer. She'd made that decision after watching us play and pushed me against a wall, her face close to mine, her eyes so wide. She came to our apartment that next day and immediately got into it with Vivian, our landlord. There was an issue with the front gate of the apartment building and the way that the gate slammed. It was so loud, it shook the entire building, and for the other tenants it was a constant thing.

"Don't. Slam. The gate."

Courtney slammed it right away. She did it immediately after being told not to. In Vivian's face and then every other time she went through it.

Her energy was chaos, like a person with too many arms. Too many words, too many points to make, her references and allusions never stopped. She was things she was not, full of contradictions. She was rich, she was poor, she had family, she was an orphan, she had friends, she had enemies. She'd tell the story you'd either want to hear or wish you could tell yourself. She lied a lot, exaggerated always. She didn't stop talking, she never listened directly but she was a sponge.

Years later she explained her method to me and it said a lot. She plucks random words or phrases from anything in eyeshot, a book on a floor, a slogan from a badge on a kid's jacket, a billboard driving by in a car, she takes a word from a coincidental periphery and works it into her trope. In real time. Her mind moves that fast.

There's a movie where Kevin Spacey constructs an entirely false narrative in a holding cell as he's being questioned and it turns out his construction is made of words he's picked up around the room, from a magazine on a desk, a flyer on a bulletin board. I like to think this method Courtney employed was her own, more original than one that could exist in a movie, but maybe it's a condition. The takeaway is that like a fast and furious tractor, she never stopped.

Courtney and I left the apartment the night she came over, the night after we met, and bought cheap alcohol from the Fairway Market on the corner. We took pills and walked and walked and climbed a fence that was near some water. Near a bread factory where the punk rock kids would go to steal loaves in the early mornings or late nights. The air smelled like toast. We sat side by side on the edge of the dirty bank and drank from the bottle. It came up we were both Cancers and she asked, "When's your birthday?" It turned out we had the same birthday. She and I were born on the same day, July 1. That connection was stunning and visceral, vivid and real, the odds were astounding.

From that point on we were connected. We celebrated our birthdays together every year. When we were both in Los Angeles, my family expected her, they'd set an extra place at the table. My mother at first couldn't stand her and would ask cautiously and skeptically, "Is Courtney coming?"

On a night after five or six years of celebrations, when I was going through her purse at a Mexican restaurant in the Mission, I found an ID of hers. She wasn't born on my birthday at all. She was born a week later, July 9. It was more remarkable than anything else.

Courtney joined the band and we had a project that pushed the she-and-me into a deeper realm. She liked to dress me, if she had her way I'd not have been a boy at all but a Victorian doll. It was a time for men to be adorned with pretty things, it just was. We had barely encountered Boy George in our lives. Traditional roles were being challenged, expanded, decorated.

As my constant, Courtney was bejeweling me and further enhancing my fucked-up rag-doll look with bracelets and earrings and the ballet-looking flats from Chinatown that women wore. It was basically me in a Mary Jane. I'd be in robes and loose hippie swaddles and she'd wear slips, undergarments, and fake fur coats, things she'd take from apartments she'd visit. We'd walk arm in arm through the Mission and she'd say, "We're cuter," to other couples who passed.

I had a Cartier watch she was obsessed with. She loved it and its middle-class reference. I let her wear it and she broke it right away. Like the gate she slammed, she couldn't help but break things. Things fell apart around her. The watch is still broken and I keep it with other saved and precious things on a shelf in my bathroom. My parents gave me and my sisters those watches when we were teenagers. My sisters think they're fake, I've never been sure.

Courtney would steal clothes from girls' closets in apartments in the village. She'd take food from refrigerators, make herself at home, swaddle into a used communal sofa, and create a mess. She'd run up phone bills on other people's phones, when long-distance phone calls cost money. "Seven digits, Courtney!" they'd yell from down the hall. She'd be in a closet with the phone talking to Minneapolis or London. She went as a phone bill for Halloween one year.

13

....

With Courtney as our singer, we became a different band. She was poetic and threw everything into her words and presentation. The tragedy, the drama, spewing out of her naturally. It was impossible to not look, her perspective was hinged and scrappy, preposterously prophetic. In any situation she commanded the room. She screamed, she performed, she pointed, she twirled, she stole, she cheated with boyfriends, she burned things, she conspired, she exaggerated, she lied, she laughed, she bragged, she was a master of words and wrote amazing poetry. She was a force, a gale, and a genius. People hated her, mostly women, but the ones like me who adored her were special. I loved her and stuck by her no matter what.

Courtney's friends were immediately family, royalty. Marie worked at Nana on Polk Street near my movie theater and I'd go and visit on my breaks. The movie would start and I'd have nearly two hours to do as I pleased, so I'd walk Polk Street and mingle with the sex workers and the addicts, get quarters for change from the private-cabin sex-booth shop and buy big cartons of cream for the coffee from the corner market. Marie was working when I first met her and wearing a Def Leppard shirt that she'd worn every day for over three weeks. This was punk rock. She had colored hair, beads in her braids, and was adorned in layers of muted textiles and tapestries. Like a soothsayer or a witch from the past with a crystal ball, but she loved Flipper. The band. We all loved Flipper. She had the first nose ring I'd seen. She was a stunning cherubian princess. She told me she'd call her father at night and just cry into the phone. He lived in Hawaii. No words, just crying into the phone. It was a testament to the extent of her pathos. Marie ended up adopting two neighbor children years later from the housing project across the street from where she lived on 14th Street in the Mission. When she got married to a tattoo artist, I gave her a butcher knife for a wedding present. The last I heard she was living with oversized potbellied pigs as pets in Sonoma, sleeping with them in her bed.

Matthew and Mark were champions of Courtney. They and their friend Ben had a fanzine called the *Bag Issue*. It was a collection of modern street poetry and that sells it short. It was inside jokes and drawings, comic strips and references to us in our bubbled culture. The three of them were dirty and adorable, younger than the rest of us. They wore old-man clothes, old-man shoes with no socks, and slept with everyone. I stayed friends with Matthew forever. We obsessed over Madonna all the way down to Los Angeles, where we moved years later, and strategized legitimate ways to get into her wedding with Sean in Malibu. Matthew eventually moved back to SF. He ended up joining the swimming club in Aquatic Park, not the one I was a member of, the fancier one, next door to it. Now he publishes a magazine of realty, a glossy presentation of buildings for sale, flats for rent, local politics, photos and portfolios of realtors. I like to think there are roots of the *Bag Issue* in it. Mark became a fireman. I don't know where Ben is. They were our band's biggest fans, mostly because of Courtney. Her energy catapulted us into a different realm. It wasn't as comfortable for Billy and Mike as it was for me. For me it felt like home, family.

It took more of an open mind for drama and theater than existed to get on board with what we were doing with Courtney. Our flavor and initial thesis we'd created before she came on board was way more driven by a masculinity that was dark and oppressive. The likes came from boys who liked bugs on the sidewalk, comic strips of grotesque street life, motorcycles and trench coats, black coffee and fingerless gloves. I'm not sure what I'm trying to say. I can list off lots of things that Courtney *wasn't*. Maybe that's not the point. She was so many more things than she wasn't.

We performed for a local nonprofit TV show, I remember the host, an enthusiastic man who wore drag sometimes but was straight. He appreciated the chemistry of the chaos we'd created. Courtney went to the flower mart early after having stayed up all night before we taped our segment. She collected garbage bags of reject flowers that were being thrown out and covered our stage with them. We had a banner that we'd hand-painted and we hung it behind us as a shrine. We were still in our dashikis and burning incense. Courtney wore her white slip, barefoot, and I remember her scraping her bare arms with the thorn of a rose as she sang, carving our band's emblem onto the inside of her arm.

We played a show at Club Foot and it was the first time I saw someone go into the bathroom to do drugs. Using the space for that purpose. Courtney locked herself in the small cubicle with Paula, a different Paula, right

before we played. It was downstairs in a basement and the
walls and stairs and ceiling were covered, completely covered, in graffiti. Club Foot was beautiful, the space was
ours, it doesn't make sense that it existed. It was perfect.
And the name. Club Foot. That space and the Tool and
Die. Names like these no longer exist. These spaces don't
exist. The impetus to create them doesn't exist.

Courtney lived in spurts. Money would come in on
the first of the month from a trust fund and she'd blow
it hugely and quickly on perfume and candles, flowers,
lingerie, drugs. It went so fast, by the beginning of the second week of the month it would be gone and she'd pout
for a day or more before dealing with having none. That
first week though.

Extravagant gestures were made when the money first
came. I remember staying in a hotel she paid for with a
window that looked out onto Carol Doda's tits. It was a
dream of Courtney's. She idolized the old stripper whose
tits blinked in a neon sign up above Broadway in North
Beach. The window opened right onto them, Courtney
had demanded that particular room. We kept the window
open and the tits blinked into the room. We left a bottle
of champagne on the sill and I knocked it off accidentally
when I got out of the bubble bath. We looked where it
fell, our two heads wet from the tub out of the window,
peering down onto the crowded sidewalk of tourists below. The barker from the club came up and pounded on
the door, screaming, and tried to kick us out. We screamed
back and got drunker. We lit scented candles and got back
in the tub with the fancy soap she'd bought.

We'd ride the bus every day. Who was on the back
of the 22 Fillmore was forever important. Mostly it was

friends or people we'd like to know. On my way home on the 22 from the first day of a job painting houses, I lost a card game with some kids and they took all my tools, I'd had no money. Years later Courtney walked offstage after her show at the Fillmore and boarded the 22 as a nostalgic gesture. Went to the back of the bus and just sat.

We'd give away flyers for our shows. I steered the artwork toward cheeky homoerotic imagery, Courtney used her loopy scrawl and cutouts of flowers and cherubs from vintage fashion magazines. Billy liked imagery of iconic symbolism. The perspective was skewed and I knew it wasn't going to last.

We were more of a gang than a band. Maybe that's why the boys turned on Courtney. The high-ended drama, the arrivals and departures capped with screams and twirling tantrums overshadowed the art and craft of what we did musically. People who came to our shows wanted to see what Courtney would do. But only in a mildly bored and jaded San Francisco way. There was a lot of drama in our scene to choose from. For the boys in the band, the interest in Courtney took away from the music. She was more fascinating than we'd be, her presence eclipsed what we presented. Billy especially resented that and Mike was quick to agree. We'd been through singers and they insisted we didn't need one. That idea to me was ridiculous but I stuck with my crew.

I remember writing her the letter and ending it with, "I hate you and I love you very much." Things never ended between us but it was over with her and the band. There wasn't a bump in our relationship, it continued its up-and-down road of faith and intolerance, it never ended, my eyes are still rolling.

I'd like to think our sex had been magnetic and powerful, but it just wasn't. It was no fault of hers. Have you ever been a gay boy and had to pretend that straight sex was a turn-on? It might have been at one point. I loved her and was enraptured. Her body was thick and solid, strong and uncompromising. Her hands which I adore were those of a sexy boy, big, fleshy, chunky. I remember her ripping down the sheet that was hung over the window next to my bed as she rode me because a neighbor was watching. She needed more than my involvement.

We broke promises and loved and lied and catapulted physically into each other. We had an abortion I wanted to be more a part of. We cried in a playground on a swing set in front of a church in North Beach. What the baby would look like, its nobility was like a future dream of passion, like fame, like notoriety, like success. Possibilities were such a tease because in our young lives anything was doable. It was near the end of the month and Courtney's money had run out. I don't know how we paid for it.

There was a romantic connection that continued for years. She'd fight fire with flares. When it was clear it wouldn't work with me, she'd flaunt new loves or fucks in my direction. There were many and I complacently adored the attention. Attention at that age felt so good. I became the victim of a lot of acting out. She fixated on a pretty boy from Madison, Wisconsin, who was gorgeous and dating Marie or someone close to her. When it didn't work out the way she wanted, she set her apartment on fire, claiming it was an accident, a candle, a curtain.

Lots of years later she married a man on a whim in Los Angeles and I spent their wedding night with her doing heroin in bed in a Hollywood apartment. The husband was at work or something? It felt like it was my own reaction to her decision to get married and I called her later that next day to tell her I loved her. I did love her but it was also just the heroin.

14

·······

Throwing things off buildings, stealing from stores, making bomb threats, taking drugs, telling lies, that was my youth, where I started from and who I became. When do we start to become what we become? It was a salad of accomplishments that we started to learn and earn in the neighborhood as children. From my sisters initially and then branching out to kinships close. The Musics on the corner, the Gibbs across the street, Bunny and Jimmy two doors down. Bunny Chambers was born without a butthole and it had to be drilled in. I can't remember how we knew that but we all did. Conversations and revelations like these were our beginnings.

We played tag in the Safeway when we were younger. I was eleven and Stephanie was nine. We'd started going there and filling up shopping carts with food we weren't allowed to have at home: sugar cereals, store-bought cookies, orange snacks in bags. We'd fill the shopping cart up and leave it there, in the aisles of the store. That was the game.

Another game was we'd move the products of the market around the store, swap the dried fruit on their shelf with real fruit, put the meat in the candy section, cleaning products in the freezer section. This to us was genius and sophisticated, so much funnier than the rest of the world.

The trick to playing tag in the Safeway was to stay

composed as you ran away from who was it. In outdoor tag
it was all scream and run, but in the confines of the store the
challenge of the game was to make your face flat and not
give anything away. Walk fast, don't run, arms close to your
sides, blending in with the other shoppers. I became best at
it when I stopped caring who knew we were playing. My
sisters kept up the ruse of composure but I'd just run and
let my face go in all different ways, using my outdoor voice
inside loudly.

Down the street from the Safeway was the hardware
store where we'd walk the aisles and set all of the alarms on
the clocks to the same time, fifteen or twenty alarms going
off together at two thirty or four. As they did we'd be gone,
farther down the street, maybe in the pet store where we'd
open all the bird cages, leaving them open to let the para-
keets fly free, or later, another time, steal salamanders out of
the aquarium, take them home, and lose them in the garden.
Across the street, in the middle of the block, a general store
where we glued things together for fun. We learned most of
what we did on that street. I could go on and on.

On the corner, down and kitty-corner from the Chambers, was the Lot where we spent a season digging a deep
pit in the dirt to hang out in and smoke. From the pit we'd
throw rocks and bottles at the buses driving by on 3rd Street
and the police would come.

There was a beehive in a bush in a corner of the Lot that
we were mad at. We suited Maureen McNally, who could fit
her whole fist in her mouth, in ski pants and a thick parka,
a motorcycle helmet and gloves. We gave her a baseball bat
to hit the hive with. Bees got up into her shirt and stung her
and she ran around the Lot and took the parka off, then her
shirt, topless, screaming and running, getting stung.

We made up games with the phone. We'd call LAX and page Robert Redford or someone famous.

"Yeah," we'd say on the phone when we did it. "It's a *different* Robert Redford, not the famous one."

That was it. That was the end of the game. We loved the idea of people's reaction to hearing, "*Robert Redford, please pick up a white courtesy phone. Robert Redford.*"

We'd also call Japan. We'd hang up before someone answered because of the long-distance charges. The game was just calling Japan, knowing we were making a sound in Japan. A noise in a country so far away.

Another game was we'd call a number just one digit off from our home number, the one we were calling from. We'd huddle around in the den, one of us crouched on the footstool, the phone cord pulled long, hand-cupped, speaking into the receiver: "Mom?"

"Excuse me?" from the person we'd called. "This isn't your mother."

"Oh no," we'd go, and lay out the scenario. "I'm . . . I'm at the movie with my friends and my mom gave me a dime to call her after the movie ended so she could come and pick us up. I think I must have misdialed, is this 934-1530?"

"No honey, this is 935-1530."

"Oh no," we'd really work it. "I dialed a 5 instead of a 4. And I just had that one dime. I don't have another one to call her now." We'd pretend to cry.

"I . . . I don't know what . . ." the stranger would say.

"Um, would you ever . . . It's just, I don't have another dime. Could you just call this number, call my mom? Tell her to pick us up? It's this," and we'd give the number we were calling from, the number one digit off from theirs.

We'd hang up and wait and they'd call back. When they did, we'd pick up the phone and scream, "Beat ya home!!!!"

The game didn't even make sense. We'd made it up.

To act out in young and undefined ways was an exercise in hysteria. Without the nonsensical and absurd we were left with flat and tedious. To an extent, it's always been about the color of the action of the kids and our community.

15

· · · · · · ·

Chuck hadn't grown up too far away. He'd been in a band with Billy in Los Angeles when we were in high school. Why we went there after we'd moved up to the village is unclear. Chuck had not a lot of a voice. He lived still in Los Angeles. He was an alcoholic and lazy and hilarious and a shambles. He believed in himself only vaguely, but the preposterous aspect of his delivery had a charm. Maybe, but no, but like . . . how could this guy . . . ?

And then he does.

He's onstage, fronting a band. There was charisma. There was style. There was bravado. There wasn't a voice and that part always felt wrong to me, but again, we weren't dealing in conventions. We were going out of our way to present a counterintuit. It was a ridiculous idea to enlist him as a singer and I got on board on that premise alone. The ridiculousness.

Regardless of my reservations, Chuck and I became friends. There was a nonchalance he exhibited that was undeniably comforting. We smoked pot together and didn't give a shit about shit. That was our consummate perspective, a constant lethargic shrug of the shoulders to any peak or valley that came our way. Quelled by weed. His habit was on a constant quest, he'd wake up early and need it. I didn't care that much but I appreciated his drive and where he'd go with it. It was high drama the way he'd engage. Searching the crevices of a living room couch, a car, the inside of the stem of a pipe. It was a forever treasure hunt for him to find weed.

I'd moved into an apartment deep in the Mission with new friends and Chuck would come up from Los Angeles for shows and stay with us. He got on well with me and my roommates who were all kids on drugs and bicycle messengers.

His arrival would constantly cut it too close, getting to town always late or minutes before the show. We'd pick him up from the Greyhound station on 7th Street. He'd get off the bus a little bit drunk, having made a friend, with an Olde English quart in a brown paper bag, smirking and embarrassed, pulling nose hairs out with his dirty fingernails, and he'd leave the next morning, after the show. He didn't like San Francisco.

Chuck didn't like San Francisco but San Francisco loved Chuck. There was a dismissive spirit to what he did. He really never cared, and what a refreshing quality/anti-quality it was to have as a front person for a band. Babies loved Chuck. That surprised me. Women loved Chuck. That surprised me too. He was filthy. I can still see him pulling out those nose hairs. His style was a carnival, a disheveled festival of colors and references, his short dreadlocks taped off with a Day-Glo-pink from a roll my sister had found on a coffee table in a café, floppy bell bottom pants, a plaid blazer from an old-man thrift store, sunglasses with an arm missing. He was cuddly and heroically relatable in a real city way. He drank too much and he smelled like bongwater and Olde English and his obsession with getting high worked in some chaotic form of what we did as a band.

With Chuck in the band we arrived at a chapter of regularity. He was a lead singer. Unlike where we'd gone before. He obliterated the parade of musical chairs. We had a lead singer in Courtney but she had wanted to do it and loved the spotlight. Chuck couldn't have cared less. He'd go through the motions of coming up from LA and do the shows, but it felt like he was just looking for ways to fuck or do drugs. It was hard to imagine him caring about anything.

The new kids who came in place of the Courtney fans were more skaters. There was a lot of skateboarding in SF. The chic crew was a team called JAKS who were sexy druggy boys, bike messengers mostly, who hung in a gang. They wore jackets with sewn-on patches of colors on their backs. Their leader was John Marsh. He was a time-less-looking, dashing, movie star of a man, really beautiful. Like *Grapes of Wrath* or James Dean. I'd clocked him working at the pizza place on Castro and then I'd see him in our mix, at shows. I watched him once at the Sound of Music high on heroin, he'd worked his arm around a post in the club, watching Flipper, and had hooked a finger through the belt loop of his pants to hold himself up as he nodded off. It was one of the first times I saw one of us on heroin.

I'd seen it around and I knew Courtney had done it. I hadn't. She and I once bought opium on the street in Chinatown and we'd done that. Someone told her the most effective way to feel the drug was to stick it up our butts, so that's what we did. I felt nothing but that's sort of the game with opiates. Everyone says, "I don't feel it."

All of the JAKS team were high on heroin and so were most of the cool bike messengers. The older musicians did dope. Jeffrey Lee Pierce we looked up to and Lou Reed from afar. It seemed like a part of growing up.

Our crew did hard drugs but people weren't yet dying. AIDS was just beginning. MaryJo was a new roommate of mine. She and her boyfriend Greg would act in my short films. They'd do drugs but wouldn't really talk about it because they knew I didn't do it. They were protecting me. No one had died yet.

We'd taken over the apartment on Harrison and 25th from a collective of activists called Bikes Not Bombs that worked getting bicycles to people in need in Nicaragua. From them we'd inherited a sofa, the kitchen table I drew on with a Sharpie, colored Mexican tissue paper cutouts we left up on the walls of the hallway. MaryJo would cook big meals, there'd be a dozen of us at the house at nighttime. JoAnn worked at a bakery and would bring home black plastic garbage bags full of day-old pastries. Fancy pastries. I barely knew what a croissant was or how to say it. We'd sit on the ratty couch in the living room and smoke pot and eat pastries straight out of the black garbage bag.

Stella was older than all of us and was always high on meth. She had hair like a haystack, black and wide like one of Marge Simpson's sisters, dark under her eyes, she was goth like most of our generation then. She'd sit in front of the TV with a jar of mayonnaise and a spoon. The rest of us ate pastries.

There were constant drugs in the apartment. Different people would sleep over, there was always someone on the couch. One of the roommates sold weed. The Butthole

Surfers were leaving once when I came home after staying out all night. Catherine from Canada moved in and sold hash oil. It was exotic. People sold different drugs but that one was unique. It came in little glass vials with tiny corks. We'd put the oil on a pin and put the tip of the pin on a heated plate. The hash oil would drip down and melt onto the plate and we'd suck up the smoke with a straw. Catherine from Canada was a bike messenger, her brother was in JAKS.

I was home in the tub taking an afternoon bath and Catherine from Canada walked in. She was high on acid and in a bathrobe. She was *too* high on acid. She wasn't making sense, speaking in riddles, weird twists of the tongue, and I just kind of went with it. I let her sit on the side of the tub with me in it. I figured being casual, all naked, would relax her. The opposite of uptight. It did relax her. She took off all her clothes. She spun down the hall naked and laughing, tearing down the colorful Mexican tissue cutouts from the walls, the tacks stuck in her hair. She was happy, it wasn't like a bad trip from a movie. She was having a good time. Before I got out of the tub she'd left the house, naked, her robe on the floor of the hallway near the front door. We looked for her late into the night and couldn't find her. We made phone calls and there were search parties of friends helping. She ended up at a campground where bike messengers without homes slept. That's the last we heard of her. One of the roommates in the house took all her hash oil and sold it.

JoAnn, the baker who brought home the pastries, was from Alabama. Mobile. She had a heroin habit and was open about it. It came from a deeper time in her past and she treated it like medicine. MaryJo was real bossy with her, they fell into a relationship like that. JoAnn lit candles in her room and one night as she nodded off her hair caught on fire and a sheet that hung from her window went up in flames. The hallway filled with smoke and we screamed and threw water at her and randomly into her room at the burning sheet.

JoAnn became close with Chuck. They had a thing, I could never tell who he was fucking. She took a photograph of our band to a psychic and she'd looked at me weird after that. The psychic had said something about me in the picture that set her off. I was holding a gun in the photo, maybe it was that, but I never learned what the psychic had told her. JoAnn wouldn't say. I'd figured it was either AIDS or big money. JoAnn's best friend from Mobile was Pip, who Chuck eventually had two daughters with, the oldest of which became my goddaughter.

Out my bedroom window in the new flat I hung an extension cord that the downstairs neighbors used to power their apartment with. They were behind on their electricity bill. There weren't enough prongs in our apartment and I'd have to unplug it sometimes to plug something else in. When I did, their lights, their TV, the kids' stereo would all fade to black and they'd shout up from below, "La bebe! The baby!" That's how they asked me for the electricity initially, to heat up the bottle for the baby.

In our backyard there was a lane called Balmy Alley that was famous for its murals. On our back gate there was a sculptural line of clothes being hung up to dry. They were real clothes, dried pants, blouses, scarves, on a clothesline that had been painted. There were messages in Spanish painted onto the clothes that I didn't really understand.

If the sun happened at all in the village, it happened in the Mission. That was where it shined first. There were palm trees and sprinklers and paleta stands that sold fruit popsicles, taco carts and women selling pupusas. Mission Street was festive and charged with traffic that slowed to bumper-to-bumper. Slow-cruising old cars and girls with big hair, tattooed necks and chinos and button-downs. Old deserted movie palaces melded into department stores and burned out businesses that never had a chance. Trash cans overflowed and schoolchildren waited in line for the buses. There was a trick of pulling the big cable that connected the electric bus to the cables that stretched over the streets. One kid would disconnect it and the bus driver would have to stop and get out and walk around to reconnect it at the back of the bus. When he did, another kid would board the bus and steal the stack of transfers to sell at bus stops.

We hung out in the local cafés. There were lots of them and we took advantage of them one by one. There weren't cafés in Los Angeles, it wasn't something that American cities did yet. There certainly wasn't special coffee anywhere, but more than the espresso or the latte or the cortado, there were the spaces we could convene. We'd drink the black coffee mostly because there were free refills and we could sit at the tables for hours, scheming and goofing and banging on things until we were asked to leave or got bored and left on our own. We'd read the message boards and spread out the free weekly on a big table and convene.

Young Vietnamese children would go from table to table in the cafés carrying bags of garlic to sell, and we taught them how to make money by taking a head of garlic out of each bag and creating an additional bag to sell for themselves.

We were political in the village, but unto ourselves, we took care of us. The 1984 Democratic Convention came to town and we were on fire with the challenge of it and what it meant to us. It was an energized summer and we all came alive, it's what the village lived for, a cause and a determined collective uprising. The tone of bands in our scene had changed from something aimlessly dark to rebels with a cause. Bands from the Vats were participating in protests around the convention. MDC. Crucifix. A band from somewhere else called Reagan Youth played. Lynn's band, the Dicks, played. Gary Floyd was a hero, he was the singer of the Dicks. He was queer and loud about it; he'd wear dresses. They all set up and played across the street from where the convention was happening. The whole city was there and there were clashes between us and the riot police. It was an uprising. Lots of us were hit with batons and arrested.

Sheilagh approached a cop at the cusp of the standoff and offered him a flower from a bunch that she carried. A cameraman from the news didn't quite catch it and asked her to do it again and she refused. Sheilagh got hired right after that to work as a security guard for the huge abandoned hospital up on the hill next to Buena Vista Park. It was the big pink building you could see from everywhere. I'd go and visit her late at night and we'd run down the empty hallways with a shopping cart, taking turns riding and pushing. I saw her years later asking for spare change on the street in front of a burrito place. I wish I could remember her last name, I'd try to find her.

Most of my friends didn't overlap. I'd learned how

to compartmentalize being gay and I stayed good at it. There were factions and chapters and sections in my life that stayed divided. My world would have benefited if I'd been able to lose those divisions, but I didn't have the tools. Instead I honed in on the eccentricities and flavors and characteristics of all the differences of all the phases and places that I felt comfortable in. I've said I was like my dad; this only became apparent to me when we buried him. There was no one he wasn't interested in. I'd thought I was like my mom because of the piano, but I was really like my dad. Open-minded sounds like bragging, but really, my mind was open, wide open. I was persuadable and open to a fault.

16

·······

'll never know the process or the horror of raising children. I won't know the fears of having gotten it wrong, the panic of loss, the not understanding, the confusion. My parents tried but were simply not equipped. My father had held the reins in the episode of my grandfather's desk but my mother was the mastermind. She kept tabs on the score, it's what she did best. Who was owed what, who deserved what, she kept track, like a hall monitor or a policewoman. On account of her red hair. It was a beacon, a badge, a siren. She'd been called ugly as a child because of it until her red hair became her. Her crown of duty, her big-lady wink of spunk and bang, she'd had no choice but to lead with it. She'd have looked good in a uniform. My father used to say he'd get one for her so she could sit at the corner of Windsor and Beverly and monitor the cars that cheated the red light. Things like that were important to her, who was getting away with what. She'd feel the back of the television when she and my father got home late at night to check whether we'd been watching it. She'd finger the bristles of our toothbrushes to see if we'd brushed. It became so rewarding to outsmart her because it meant so much to her to be right.

Los Angeles was big, big league for her, water so deep. She spun in an unfamiliar world she didn't know. She was a small-town girl from Wall, South Dakota. In the big city, references and recommendations and tutelage at how to make it work were on hand certainly. She had magazines and friends and the wives of other of my father's friends who were struggling, like her, to find their way. She learned things from others, sharp and absorbent, but mostly she figured it out on her own. To me she was and would always be a dazzling heroine, a grand and strengthened pioneer woman of the Midwest. A rein in a single hand, a prairie dress, her red bun coming out of a bonnet in strands, face dusty with trials and errors, eyes fierce and determined, skeptical and guarded, poised in a foreground, disregarding the squalls and tumbleweeds behind her, open slightly to suggestion but drawn ultimately to the direction of morale.

Before the cooking classes, before the chicken Kiev, before the gauchos and Mary Tyler Moore, she took a course somewhere hosted by a color specialist who let her know that her colors were earth tones. What worked best for her natural coloring and genetic makeup were earth tones. That's what she paid to learn and we all respected that. From then on it was only oranges, dusts, browns, and rust, her favorite. Her look evolved to sassy and sophisticated. A sheep vest. Frye boots, a medallion belt with inlaid turquoise. She got a perm. Her spirit was wild, swathed in inspirational gestures cultivated from fashion and gardens, magazines, royalty. As she evolved she held on to her queerness, part of her, like her red hair.

Her flair, her relentless patrolling of justice, her taste and conviction, it all ended up tangled in a bun on the church floor. She'd make decisions and take directions that I respected but they'd be cloaked in the church. It wasn't until I was much older that I realized all the St. Anne's girls, the ones who'd come and stayed and taken care of us as kids, were young women living out their terms of pregnancy. They were all pregnant. Maybe it was just cheaper, simply a solution of economy, nannies for free, I don't know, but ultimately I found the slightly sadistic gesture of taking in girls and forcing day care on them genius.

The real bond between mother and son was the music. She had perfect pitch, she could play any song in any key on the piano. With me, my mother had a protégé and an inspired musical confidant. My sisters would have continued with the piano had it been up to my mother, but none of them felt the music the way I did. It's a statistic I quote to young parents on a quest, developing musical offspring: "The music gene will stick with one out of four," basing my theory on how it went down with my sisters, compared to me. They say the relationship between the son, particularly the only son, and the mother is unrivaled. Yes, it was. We had that. Adding music to that equation upped our relationship to one of crazed and sweet furor.

Like a crusader, she worked her way into a group who went to the prison downtown every Sunday for a Catholic mass. She did this every week for over twenty years, played the piano for the prisoners. It wasn't a feeble undertaking and it showed more strength than I'd known she had. She'd drive downtown and park underground and go through security checks and touch prisoners at the sign of peace, take their hands and look into their eyes. This was her favorite part. They weren't allowed to touch each other but they could touch my mother. They were hardened men, rapists, murderers, all of them looking for forgiveness. The prisoners loved her. One flashed her once, pulled out his cock and flaunted it insanely in the mass; she was quick to forgive and laughed it away. There was a prison riot that erupted during the mass one day, and as the fighting started in the chapel and the gangs threw punches and chairs at each other, she continued to play her piano, even when the priest told her to stop. Long after my father died and into her final chapter, she lived that life, holding men's hands, offering solace and saying, "Peace be with you."

I'd be grounded forever, I kept getting caught. Weeks or months, like a cloistered nun in captivity. There were attempts by my parents to set me on a better path. Me in the front seat of the car with my father. He'd taken the day off from work to try to fix things with us. He had been seeing a therapist. My parents both had. I knew without being told that this was an idea from the therapist: one-on-one time with the troubled son. My father had taken me on a day trip to the mountains and for some reason we didn't make it out of the city. I was midway through my punishment, my penance, pouting, doing the silent treatment. I'm realizing now how long I've been doing that. The game of the passive passenger, not speaking and giving small answers. I still do it and it's as effective as it's always been, which is to say *not*. Not at all. These are the unfortunate times I want back with my father. He in the driver's seat, trying. Me in the passenger seat, silent. There are so many things I could have said. If I knew then what I know now.

It's an exercise of restraint and humiliation to keep quiet and not say enough. At some point I stopped expressing my truth and led with a lie. The lie was who I thought I needed to be, a boy running wild in the world with other boys, normal boys who dated girls, boys who survived on boy things and ate boy diets, boys whose knees got scuffed and boys who led with aggression, boys who led with a bully fist and ignored the pretty. It was the opposite of the me that existed, the flip side of who I was at my core. I buried the me that flowered and tried to cultivate a me that did the things I had no interest in doing.

There were exceptions and I'd worked the loopholes in my punishment. Things I'd claim I'd need to do. The library. Technically, the terms of my punishment allowed me to visit the library and neighbors in the radius of our block. I'd say I was going to these places and then I'd run briefly free. Opportunities like these I'd jump on, take advantage of, or just stuff my bed with pillows and sneak out the window. My drug buddies would take me in with wide-open arms, welcoming me back, citing the days it had been since. I'd go back to my cruising spots when I could.

My sisters were my refuge, my holy grail, royalty. The three of them are closer to each other than they've ever been to me. They are witches and they communicate without words. They taught me games: Bloody Mary in the Mirror. Light as a Feather, Stiff as a Board. Seances. The Ouija board. They taught me how to put my hair up in a turban, how to twist the towel and make it stay. They share recipes with themselves and with me when I ask.

There is a connection I missed out on as a boy, but their initial intent was to raise me as one of them. That happened and then it didn't. They currently each have matching necklaces, three necklaces with three beads on them. They found them recently on a trip I wasn't on. I'm not one of the beads. I asked innocently if I could be the third bead when one of them dies. It's funny, but only to me. They feel bad about the exclusion.

We did a performance in bikinis when we were young to the "Yellow Polka Dot Bikini" song for our parents' friends at a cocktail party in the living room of the old house and I didn't understand how it was funny. The funny wasn't what we were going for. My sisters had encouraged me and I was excited to be part. The bikini fit so well, the thong of it so snug. I ran out of the living room when I realized it was wrong and I was being laughed at.

Catherine, the oldest sister, tutored me. Shorts weren't cool. Tan was cool, shorts weren't, so my pale legs were complicated. Calling our parents Mom and Dad was preferable to Mommy and Daddy. I wasn't sure where it was all going but I did my best to follow her course and imitate her. I wasn't allowed but I listened to her records and put them back where they belonged so I wouldn't be caught. Neil Young, Cat Stevens, Jackson Browne, David Bowie. She was a rebel and a pioneer, the firstborn. She trampled the roughage of a trail and plundered it on her own. Flattened the terrain for herself all alone. She was the first to get caught shoplifting, the first to run away, the first to use drugs. She hid her rolling papers behind the drawer on the inside of her bureau in her closet. She had a Charlie Brown diary that I wasn't supposed to read. She had a bathroom window that she'd sit on the ledge of and smoke cigarettes in her navy-blue school uniform. She pinned me down and dripped a slow saliva into my face until I parroted back what she wanted me to say. She became a political activist and got arrested for protesting.

I adored her and I would do anything for her attention.

Elizabeth, the second sister, whistled and tap-danced. She was attached to the rest of us but quietly persevered alone through childhood. She had a skin condition on her hands, and the sides of her feet and her face would transform in a rapture as she scratched at them, satisfying the itch. Her mouth would twist and she'd look to a faraway place. She had just the one friend, Eileen Pryor. That changed to Elizabeth Papillion, later to Maura McCarthy, always just one at a time. She would wear her long green nightgown and when it got cold she'd stand above the floor heater, filling it up with hot air like a huge bell. When Cora, the Mexican daughter of a couple who my parents met on a plane, came and visited for a week, I told her, when asked, that Elizabeth was my favorite. Elizabeth had told her the same about me. Cora revealed that to the both of us in the back of the car coming home from ice cream. I was holding a soggy piece of wafer cone, hiding it in the palm of my hand because it was preferred to be the last one holding with our treats. Elizabeth saved everything. "I licked it all!" she'd shout after Halloween. Otherwise we'd steal her candy from the pillowcase after we'd all finished ours.

Stephanie was a gymnast. She was my pet and my protégé, my partner and companion, a spectral genius of pragmatism and intuit. She worked early on at a flower shop and cultivated friendships with gay men, old people, and characters of the street. She met exotic girls, Jewish twins, Angie Dickinson's daughter, at the Beverly Hills YMCA where we'd take her for training with her gymnastics team, the Eagles. She had the free spirit and fervor of the youngest child. We eventually had a balance beam that stayed on our front lawn. Stephanie could do a back handspring on it. She coached me and worked with me but I couldn't get it, my back just wouldn't arch the way hers would. I'd cut my fingernails and my toenails and give her my clippings, a special ritual. Later, when I moved away, I'd send them to her in an envelope. It was our thing. We got high together for her first time in Westwood and we saw a movie. We took a bus home down Wilshire Boulevard at night and Stephanie had a bad reaction to the weed. She put her head on my shoulder as we rode and I was scared. The lights out the windows of the bus were flashing and too loud. That was when I used to protect and take care of her. It all changed.

17

·······

I continued to have a real disdain for Los Angeles but I'd end up there again and again. There was so much to prove going back. I'd changed and become what my upbringing was not. Letting Los Angeles know what Los Angeles was not was important to me.

I worked through a summer typing at my father's law office. My sisters worked there too. I wore a beret that held my dreadlocks up in a hidden bun. We'd go out at night and see bands and come home late. We'd take a bus in the morning, get stoned, and go to work. The sisters would alternate taking naps under my desk in the crawl space where my legs went while I typed. I'd sit and transcribe Dictaphone tapes my father had made. There was a machine that I operated with my foot, rewinding just enough to catch what I'd missed. Me with the headpiece in my ear, so close and intimate, I'd lose myself in his voice and his passion, speaking emphatically, arguing his points, while my sisters crouched tangled and sleeping at my feet.

Chuck lived in LA in a trailer in his parents' driveway and they barely tolerated him. He worked at a flower shop called Flowers That Bloom in the Spring, Tra La. I'd call him there repeatedly because he'd have to answer the phone and say the name of the shop, "Flowers That Bloom in the Spring, Tra La," and I'd laugh. When he

wasn't working we'd drive around at night endlessly looking for weed. We'd sit low in the front seat of the shitty
cars we'd borrow, taking corners wide, smoking side by
side in sunglasses, sipping Big Gulps from the 7-Eleven.
Casting a loose net in the still of a boring summer, the
yield was next to dead, very little came back.

We'd go up and back so many different ways. San
Francisco. Los Angeles. San Francisco. The Greyhound.
The midnight flyer that we'd line up for at the airport that
was twenty-five dollars. Mostly we'd drive. We'd get on the
101 as it loped out of Hollywood winding past the Bowl,
looking for its direction past the last palm trees, past Ca-
huenga, past the John Anson Ford, there on the right, the
north bearing mundanity doesn't kick in till after the valley, once we're on the 5, and past Magic Mountain. And
then, even then, there's a promise of a road that could be
someone. The grapevine appears, sudden and brazen, the
Tehachapis shoving their shoulder into the flatness of the
stolen land like a spent volcano in the dumdum desert, a
series of soft peaks so stubborn and permanent we had
to go over. The Christo umbrellas had been there not that
season but the one before, and a woman had been killed
installing the artwork, not only here but a man also, installing on the mountain range in Japan, had been killed.
They had been yellow, the umbrellas on the grapevine,
but the ones north of Tokyo had been blue. "Well worth
it," we had cheered about the installers who'd been killed.
Not cruel, not insensitive, we'd have given our own lives
for the art. Respect.

There were too many of us in a van, no seats in the
back, just the awkward and cold metal of the car that we
spread a too-small serape on and leaned on the bags and

sacks full of things we'd brought. An acoustic guitar out of its case, a paper sack of carrots, a liter of Mountain Dew, damp socks hanging and drying. Gary sang David Bowie songs, ones from *Hunky Dory*, mimicking precisely. Gary was crooked and dressed like a witch, his shoes were pointed and buckled, his cape was purple and black. The van was his but he wouldn't drive it, it was on loan and would be taken back before long so we'd made the most of the loan. We were driving it to San Francisco on a Friday. There was a party at the apartment that Courtney would eventually burn down and we were aiming to get there before midnight.

Gary was the singer in a band that Chuck and I loved called Celebrity Skin. Their craft was odd and twisted and so far wrong and mischievous and genius that it scared most people off. I'd seen a Christmas show in which they'd ensembled a collection of reindeer on cables that were pulling a Santa Claus in a sleigh in front of the stage, but the reindeer were carcasses somehow, made of old meat and goat heads. Another time after they'd finished making early demos of their songs, they played the recorded songs over the speakers and lip-synched the entire set to an audience, unaware. Later they'd befriended my sister when my parents were out of town. I lived in San Francisco by then. They convened at our family house and went through the closets and wore her high school uniforms for the show. On and on they were unparalleled, unique, and a lopsided circus of wrongs. Tim Ferris changed his name to Sugarpie much later, he wore pink tights under rips and black engineer boots, stickers on his face and ribbons in his hair. We'd heard of each other and our likeness and were friends before we met.

In the second half of the 5, past the stinky cows that were herded together in spaces too small that stretched forever and smelled so bad before they were milked or killed or used, there was Pea Soup Andersen's, a restaurant that somehow attracted travelers at the midway point with the audacious and ridiculous pitch of "All the pea soup you can eat." We were drawn to it, that pitch, and filed into the restaurant like a carnival, colors and rips and loud and practically cartwheeling to a table among the fellow travelers, so fatly drab in their journeys.

We made an immediate connection with a teenaged waitress named Carol, bored out of her mind on a Friday night, chewing gum and watching the world drive by. We asked her, "Carol, what is the most amount of bowls that have been eaten under this deal?" She told us nine and we set out to beat that number. Nine bowls was the amount we were competing with. We supped the soup vigilantly and aggressively and it kept coming. Carol had never seen anything like it. She was rooting for us. Other waitresses took note and crowded around our table. The chef peeked out from the kitchen and gave us a thumbs-up. We all finished more than five bowls and Gary went up to seven but that was it. Bloated with the green soup, we left the restaurant in a sheepish defeat. We put our money together on the table before we left, set aside an amount for the gas we'd need, and left the rest, over a hundred and twenty dollars, as a tip for Carol.

The smell of the soup, still crusted on our lips and sloshing in our stomachs, was disgusting and wrong, and Gary threw up in the parking lot as we walked to the van. Vomit is contagious and the rest of us, one by one, joined him. We were laughing and screaming and vomiting and

made a dance, a choreography of the act, spinning, cater-
wauling, leaping in the air, actually, and sticking the point
of the dance with a vomiting expulsion of the soup. I've
never laughed so hard; falling and crying, lying on the
concrete of the parking lot, we wiped ourselves clean and
got back in the van, got more gas, and drove to the party
in San Francisco, arriving after midnight and finding a
parking spot right in front of the apartment building.

We'd all graduated to a place of boring periphery in
the world. We hadn't earned the focus we aimed for but
we were all on the edge of something. Bigness and notoriety felt touchable and tangible. People close to us were
coming up and making noise. I auditioned for Public Image Ltd that summer because Pat Smear did. Courtney
was staying with him in Los Angeles and there was a public audition for the band. Courtney had put everything
she had into an audition for the role of Nancy Spungen.
She'd been right. She was absolutely perfect for the part.
There's no one who would have been better. She threw
herself into it and tantrummed her way through an audition. The role didn't happen but she got a smaller role,
one she didn't want.

The PiL audition was at Perkins Palace in Pasadena. I
took off from my dad's law office during lunch. John Ly-
don was curled up in a road case the way my sisters and
I would nap. I was pretty certain I'd get the job because I
had dreadlocks and I didn't care, but I didn't get the job
and neither did Pat. It's what we did and what Los Angeles inspired in us, to reach for unreachable things and to
fail and to keep trying and failing.

We navigated California that summer and steered the

band toward some semblance of fruition. We got to a place where we were performing the same things again and again. Songs formed into set lists. Road maps that started to follow a regularity in our shows. We hadn't referred to them as songs when we started. We were fighting the notion of convention so hard. They became songs when Courtney started mostly, and we really were getting close and comfortable with the MTV. Not up close and personal but as fans from afar. By that point we'd reference the behemoth among ourselves and out in the city, we'd do it just to piss people off. We played Van Halen's "Jump" flawlessly. It was kind of a glorious coming together of who we weren't and where I assumed we'd never go.

Chuck screamed and moaned mostly, and as literary a person as I considered myself, I really didn't pay attention to his lyrics or what he was saying. He wasn't as overtly poetic as Courtney. It wasn't until we went into the studio and recorded what we were doing that I took pause and listened. "*Over the hills, they came from the valley making innuendos 'bout my lack of talent.*"

With nothing left to do, we put some money together as a band and recorded two songs in a crusty old studio in Hollywood. One song we recorded came from a loop we'd created of the same guitar chord repeated over and over and over and over. The notion and the execution were preposterous and the song was called "Greed." There was a mechanical, maniacal beat that came in over it and eventual heaven on keyboards, but it started with that riff of repetition. That had become our credo. Beyond anything it was ridiculous and profound. With Chuck at the helm, his voice and our goals. I played it for my mom.

She tried to be encouraging but I could tell her heart wasn't so into it.

We intended to make a dance mix out of one song only because that was a preposterous notion. We recorded and mixed two or three songs and we sent them around to people. Nothing happened and no one cared. It's the heaviest of burdens when no one cares. Honestly, anything but that. Hate me or get mad at me but don't ignore me, don't not care. To keep going at that point is difficult, it's the thing of response when people ask what it takes to succeed. At that low point, in the shadows when no one cares and you can't even get a clap, you continue to work. You keep at it because you believe in yourself.

We compiled the recorded songs with some live performances of our sets and some drug-fueled sessions from our rehearsal studio onto a cassette. We figured inundation to be a key. We had created a banner with the star we'd been using. Mike spray-painting the star on a big white sheet out on our back porch where a pot of beans had been sitting for over a month was photographed by Joan. We used that image for the cover art of our cassette project. We took the cassette to a library and made over a hundred copies on a high-speed cassette copier we'd found. We folded the artwork around the cassettes and put them into long plastic envelopes. The sound quality was bad, it could only have been bad, but it was a calling card. The odds were so clearly stacked against us, we'd stacked them ourselves.

18

·······

There was a sound and a tone in that season that was fresh and new and electric. I heard it on the boardwalk at Venice Beach, coming out of a boom box, and I chased it so I could hear more. It was absolutely staggering to me. "The Message" by Grandmaster Flash and the Furious Five on the radio was a miracle. There was a quality to that sound, a mix of old electro-drum machine with the soul and the delivery of rap. It was truly a moment and I felt it first that summer. When Run-D.M.C. added their heavy guitar to the mix we were flabbergasted. It was everything. It was bombastic and rebellious, a distant cousin, a collision of worlds, a shout of spirit. It prompted me to write the lyrics to "We Care a Lot," and then things really changed.

I heard it right away as it came together. There are things you're good at it and things you're not. Something in that song was my prowess, the thing I did well. It was catchy and sarcastic and funny and empowering all at the same time. Sarcastic and sincere, disrespectful and appreciative, flippant and attentive. Chuck recognized it too. It opened doors immediately.

There was a woman in the San Francisco underground scene who none of us knew. Her name was Ruth and she wrote for *Maximum Rocknroll*, which was kind of the bible of all things legitimate in the world of punk rock.

She was a gatekeeper and strict and very SF and active in real politics in a way that we weren't. She had worked for Jello Biafra's label around the time of the censorship trials and was starting her own label. Her role in that piece of history, defending the Dead Kennedys' artwork and ultimately Robert Mapplethorpe, was tantamount to anything we'd been hoping to achieve. *We Care a Lot* became the first album on her label and she paid for us to finish recording what we'd started in the studio.

In the loneliness and shadows of creating, sometimes it's just one voice. One lone voice of encouragement. We want that, we need that, the pat on the back, the recognition that we're doing something right. It doesn't come from parents a lot of the time and we look for it in other places. When it isn't there, life feels futile and impossible. When it comes, things happen.

The studio we recorded in was over the Golden Gate Bridge in Marin. It was very cocaine. Cocaine wasn't something we ever did, it was just a Marin vibe. We were fueled in the studio by stories of Huey Lewis who'd recorded there and inside scoops on drug use and Bay Area lore that didn't really matter to us. We listened off-handedly but we really didn't care.

The song "We Care a Lot" was everything to me that we'd worked for. It was a ridiculous mix of the place we were leaving and where we wanted to go. The chunka-chunka of the guitar, the gang vocals, the syncopation of the drum and the bass, and the heaven of keys on top. It had all the ingredients coupled with the sarcastic anthem of who we weren't. Immediately, that's how it happened. People heard that song and it changed everything. We *became* that song. We were the world.

From there it all happened real fast. Not success and not money but a propulsion. The gear shifted and we started to move at a different speed. There were friends around we hadn't had before, local favors were granted, and opportunities came, but we stayed fickle and proud. Things that came our way we turned our backs on. The notion was if they didn't like us before, then now was too late.

19

....

Things happened for us and then they didn't. The impatience of living young. The expectations are ramped up and indignant. The need for now is constant. The green grass on the other side is a taunt and a tease and insufferable. Coming into my own was like a second puberty, a need for a rush of anything that would change the course of constancy. I was also sitting in my own skin and it itched. Whatever will come and where will it go? I wasn't where I wanted to be. My friend James told me, "Go someplace and things will happen." It was kind of like that.

When the record came out we went on tour. It straight-up was what was done at the time. We found a '66 Dodge truck, it was orange, and we connected a trailer to the back of it where we kept all our gear. I don't remember blankets or sleeping bags or pillows. I'd convinced the band to take my boyfriend, Jim Olson, on the road with us. How that happened I don't know. There may have been no other options. He wasn't only useless, he was a hindrance. He couldn't change guitar strings, he was indignant and an intellectual bully, I loved him but he was impossible to get along with. He was wired for contrary, always pointing out the option that no one would get on board with. It was comforting for me, in my queer world, always having the straight direction challenged, to be witness to that over and over and over. I could sit complicit and silently applaud the conflict.

I was so proud when we ran out of gas on the grapevine, the lonesome stretch of the 5 between Los Angeles and San Francisco. The gas gauge in the truck was broken so it was impossible to know how much was left, but Jim had preemptively filled a can and stashed it in the back part of the truck. There had been a resistance from the rest of the band to bringing him on the road, him not knowing how to change guitar strings and all. When we used the gas from the can, I was like . . . "See?"

We barely made any money and gave ourselves ten dollars a day each to live on. It was more than enough and I saved what I didn't spend in a dirty plastic bag in my oversized suitcase. We'd have ways to stretch the per diems, games as old as time. The food from backstage would go far. Boxes of crackers and bags of potato chips. Not-ripe fruit and bottles of things. It was amazing to me that people in other cities showed up to see us. There was no Internet and we used big square pages of paper called maps that folded up to get us from place to place.

We headed east into the summer and the drives were outrageous. In Texas we found a direction on the map that looked like a shorter distance between where we were and where we were going, off the main road. It started out as a highway and changed into dirt at a point where it was too late to turn back. It was late at night and our brights were on. There were no lights around us and everything was dark except what was immediately in front of us. We saw a rabbit, then two, then lots. Rabbits started jumping into the beams of our headlights, attracted by the glare.

At first we tried to avoid them and not hit them but we ended up just pummeling hundreds of rabbits throwing themselves into our path.

I think of those rabbits. Their pointlessness, their blind ambition, their direction, and how it came about. Did one of them make the first move? And the rest followed? The stakes were high, it was life and death. And why was Texas so big? Honestly, the size and the immensity of the state, the world was stretching on and on and we were so small in it. It came down to the six of us in a car; how did it happen that we didn't all die?

Billy and I had been friends through grammar school, Boy Scouts, and the nuns. We'd skateboarded and vandalized and grew up together. He had more of a conscience than I did and he felt bad about doing bad things. He was the oldest child and had a built-in sense of responsibility.

I'd called the Safeway when I was twelve and asked to speak to the manager. The market was three blocks from my house. I told the manager on the phone simply and directly that we'd planted a bomb in the store. Billy tried to pull the phone away from me as I swiveled around on the stool that used to be in front of the piano, turned my back to him, and pressed my forehead into the wall. I finished the call, speaking deliberately, making my voice low, my eyes squinted and serious, and placed the phone dramatically back in its cradle. Billy didn't want to but I insisted we walk up to the Safeway. The store had been cleared out, there was yellow tape surrounding the huge space of the parking lot, police cars and a bomb squad scattered up the street. The lights of the police cars were on and spinning but the sirens were quiet, their doors mostly open. The drama I'd created was a revelation. Things can happen when you put your mind to it. I walked straight up to the manager of the store and asked him what was up.

I've heard it said that at some point in your life you no longer meet people who don't remind you of someone you've already met. It happens, the similarities, certainly, but I've never met anyone like Billy. His theatrics, his storytelling, his excitement, his quest for queer flavor. My sister said he made drinking water sound fascinating.

On the road, on that first tour, Billy had held the purse strings, he made the phone calls, his opinion he'd share first. He dressed the part, carried a briefcase and wore a blazer. We all knew the blazer was wrong but applauded it. It was just like us. He handled the money and doled out the per diems. He spoke business in a way I didn't. He had studied political science. There were things missing in the rest of us that he compensated for. He appreciated the chaos that we churned and the fervor that spun around us but he had a limit as to how much he'd do or invest himself in. Which is not to say he's uptight, he's not. He's spontaneous and unpredictable and surprising. Decisions he'd make, stances he'd take, priorities he'd get behind, they were always surprising.

The paths and the fixways from us to the rest of the country were a mix of ugly American shopping malls, waterbed stores, parking lots, pizza places, gas stations, and convenient stores, laid out forever and ever across the course of our city-to-city. We'd stop to call the venue from a pay phone and get directions to the club. We'd get there and unload our equipment and nestle into our soundcheck. It was the summer and we'd sit in shorts on the long back bench of the Dodge, our sticky legs bumping against each other, and fight about the directions, the logistics, the radio station, anything that mattered.

Jim, the guitar player, was a tyrant and a bully. He made himself laugh, he had that kind of confidence. He intimidated us. His breed was exotic and foreign. He was from Hayward and real redneck. Like trucks and rifles and macaroni and cheese. He was the opposite of me, it couldn't have been written more poetically. He had grown up with three brothers, I'd grown up with three sisters. At one point in a physical fight with him in the back of an oversized truck, the air impossibly muggy, our fighting bodies dirty and slippery, his black oily hair tangled through the fingers of my clenched fist as I straddled him, he shouted like a battle call, "RAISED BY WOMEN! RAISED AS WOMAN!" It stopped the fight, the rest of us screamed, astounded and amused. I was flattered.

He was a frail skeleton of a man, brittle-boned but set like stubborn stone or petrified wood. Masculine rings and badges attached to his leather vest, the same man-boots that never changed. To be honest, I kind of loved him. I hated him for sure too, but I was in awe of his demeanor and commitment. We drove long drives together later on when no one wanted to tackle overnights with the gear truck. He and I would do it together, no problem. There was a point on a long drive when a sound came from underneath the carriage of the truck, a loud noise, deafening like metal on metal, and we couldn't get it to stop. When it was my turn to drive and I took the wheel, he reached over from the passenger seat and held his hands over my ears so I didn't have to hear it.

Randomly, Jim the guitar player accused Billy of not doing a proper job with the finances on tour, letting things slide. The rest of us wouldn't participate in the confrontation. I had no interest in following the money or the administration of what we were doing. I might have been a little bit lazy, but honestly, I just couldn't be bothered. Billy relinquished the briefcase at the end of the fight and let Jim have at it. Jim was an asshole and screamed at us always. It's surprising we all put up with it. His main target was Mike, the drummer. They'd had a past we weren't privy to. We laughed behind our hands and didn't discourage the abuse. It's not sweet to look back on.

Mike was special and unique. He was tentatively gentle and obnoxiously relentless. We were all one of a kind, honestly, but Mike was truly unto himself. He was damaged somehow on the inside from childhood. His sister I'd called Sleepy, she'd always be yawning and in and out of a bedroom in saggy clothes, she was part of the damage. They were like gnomes from a cabin in the woods. Mike's home was volatile but invisibly so. His passion for what he did was scary, he wasn't able to turn it off. His drums and his power behind them were mighty and unrivaled. He was like no one else, an anomaly, a genius. He set up his drums so they were difficult to play, not easier, he needed that challenge. The velocity with which he attacked his instrument was painful, it hurt the rest of us. It was an irreplaceable ingredient, the foundation in what we created, and he was a man of magic.

It's too much to ask of young people at that age, but the stepping up and acceptance of the job at hand made us what we were. The personalities involved were ingredients that didn't mix. We were proud and uncompromising and bold and stubborn, and our tenacity propelled us across the country. Suspecting and sarcastic and challenging and nonchalant in expectations, we pushed ourselves on the people, not expecting results so much as demanding them.

As we toured across the country, everything hinged on New York. There was a man there named Steven Barrymore Blush who we hadn't met. He'd arranged a show for us at the World and promised to pay us $1,000. It was unheard of. One thousand dollars. We talked about it as we drove, that $1,000.

Shows as we traveled and headed east would fall apart. We'd arrive to cancellations in remote cities. In the middle of everything we got stuck in Atlanta. We played a show at the Metroplex. It was a lonesome building all by itself along some train tracks next to downtown. The building was covered with graffiti inside and out. There was a man named Paul, they were all so good to us. We stayed at the Metroplex for almost a week and waited. We cut our ten dollars a day down to four dollars a day, we had run out of money.

We would set up our instruments on the Metroplex stage and play music in the afternoons before bands arrived to sound check. I remember not wanting to bother but then being happy we did. There was a song that became classic to us that we worked out on that stage. The club liked us. Bands came and went through the week. There was a sexy band called Youth of Today who were skinheads. They didn't drink or smoke and were vegetarians. Truly exotic. There were rats and the smell of shit and beer and disinfectant.

We all took Ecstasy one night. None of us knew what it was. All of us looking up at a not-quite-full moon and Paul from the club saying, "Know what? Let's just call it full." As the Ecstasy hit us we were all sitting side by side on the two bench seats of the Dodge and I said, "Who's got the keys?" It was the constant fear and question because there was only one set. The panic set in fast. Us chanting in a fervor, "Who's got the keys? Who's got the keys?" Seriously scared and agitated in our frenzy, and I realized they were in my clutched and sweaty hand. I said, "I've got the keys," and then more assuredly as if to calm a tantrummed child, "I've got the keys." The panic stopped. "He's got the keys," someone said, and then someone else, soothed and placated. "He's got the keys." I only did Ecstasy that once. It's very much that drama that sums it up for me. Not in a bad way at all. First wonder, then horror, and then the relief that everything is okay.

We left the Metroplex and got to the East Coast. Steven Barrymore Blush had a girlfriend, Sherri, who went to school in New Jersey where we played a show. We called Sherri and her friends the Volcano Sisters because they loved the band Volcano Suns. When the band stayed overnight with them after the show, Jim, my boyfriend, and Chuck and I went to New York. Jim and I went to my sisters' apartment in Brooklyn initially. Our shoes smelled so bad my sisters made us put them out in the hallway. Chuck went to his friend Anne's apartment in Alphabet City.

Chuck had a crew of friends in New York who all lived in the Lower East Side. You know what it looked like, you've seen pictures of the chain-link fences and empty lots and trash-can fires. Anne and her apartment on East 6th Street were the epicenter of the crew. The constraints of a life in New York City, the physical limitations I'd never considered. Like making the small tray work on an airplane, the one that folds down in front of you, accommodating everything it takes to eat a meal. There's enough room, it's just how you use it. Anne's apartment was over-stuffed with papers and records, fabric and costumes, skateboards and high heels and wigs, everything on top of itself and overflowing onto everything else. Heaps and piles and stacks of remnants and souvenirs and memories falling off shelves, out of closets, off the walls.

"Just move something," she'd say. I'd never seen New York. This was how it was done.

Anne and her crew had a big open space they all shared on Avenue C called Home Living. They made things there, the walls were all stenciled, there were mannequins ev-erywhere and a big sheet suspended from the ceiling, be-hind which we could sleep on the ground. The toilet was exposed to the rest of the space, I don't know how we shit. The streets outside on Avenue C were mayhem, like a village in wartime. There were fires on corners, people sleeping on sidewalks. We saw a cop on a corner as we walked and double-checked ourselves stopping at a red light, even though cars weren't coming.

"Cross the fucking street," the cop said.

Everyone in New York City made things. Skateboards and clothes and props and art and jewelry, but mostly music. I made friends for life. Anne, Jon E. Edwards, Jean, still my best friend in New York City. I owe these trea-sures to Chuck. We played the World and it was a circus, that night it was the center of the universe.

A friend in the mix was Carlo, who hosted art gathers. He had just put on a show with an artist named Martin Wong and showed me a photograph by an artist named David Wojnarowicz. It was a herd of buffalos stampeding and throwing themselves off a cliff. I'll never forget the image. He insisted I buy it, the notion of investable art going way over my head. I loved the image but it was over a hundred dollars.

There's still a feeling I get when I remember what New York City was. It was possible to be invisible, but just as possible to be magnified a million percent at the same time. The people we met were astutely aware of the score. The scrutiny and the perception of the kids on the streets was so sharp and casual. The men looked at men and the women looked at men and the men looked at women, the fashion of the people put out in a big way. Big-big gestures and just enough words to get by, economizing conversations. Not as much needed to be said. The clubs and the streets were like Anne's apartment, overstuffed and filled with ephemera.

The World was different. It was a club that was personal and unfamiliar at the same time, like a fucked-up old palace we shouldn't have been allowed in, misplaced and gone gloriously wrong. There were chandeliers, lots of gold leaf and a balcony, red carpet and elegant, delicate wainscoting that stretched the perimeter. They said that the janitor was a junkie and lived in the coat check. I saw two old ladies doing cocaine on a table, sitting next to two homeboys in baseball jerseys and a drag queen lingering alone on a pillar gyrating and working it like a pole. The club was packed when we played. It had the air of no one listening or paying attention, but everyone was. Nothing got by anyone.

Run-D.M.C. were at the show. Madonna. Hobbled-together looks of abundance in the club built from nothing. Kids wore things from the street, like literally, a parking cone for a hat, a string of flags wrapped around as a dress, cigarette butts for earrings. The language we spoke was one I immediately embraced. Hot breath in ears and sweat and urgent, we pushed against each other and solidified friendships quickly and resonantly. There was a nonchalance in the meetings we made, like strangers but old friends you'd immediately take for granted. We kissed people we shouldn't have, we smoked more than we ever had, we tried new drugs. It was a choice where to go with it. You could walk away from it or you could embrace it and throw yourself into the mix. New York City was glorious.

On my way back to Avenue C by myself after the show, I crossed the street in front of a cab that had stopped for me. There was no one in the cab, just the driver. I looked at him and he looked back. Slowly he lifted his hand off the steering wheel, and with his other hand pulled out a rubber glove. He held his hand up where I could see it and put the rubber glove on, never breaking eye contact.

We stayed up till the morning in Home Living and danced and drank and threw up and crashed. We slept on the floor and blocked out the windows when the sun came through. We left the city with our $1,000, sunburnt with experiences, and drove dumbstruck in a daze to Florida.

20

· · · · · · · ·

I'd never been there, and at first glance Florida is an oasis. The sand on the beach is that texture and color you've seen, heard about. Fine and sparkling, white and smooth, stretching flatly forever. The water is a color you'd never think ocean could be, see-through, perfection. You get in, though, and there's jellyfish. And they sting. And you gotta pee on yourself to make it better.

We played a show in Tampa and asked for a living room to sleep in from the stage. Did anyone have a couch or some floor space? It was what usually worked. A hotel, one room for the six of us, was a luxury. We'd do that sometimes but rarely, all crash together and steal the pillows.

Jim and I would sleep in the back of the Dodge. Like the back of a pickup truck but it was covered with a shell. Back there with us was everyone's luggage and miscellaneous things we'd picked up on the road. We'd sleep and fuck among it all, never bothered, in fact it was a luxury. The suite. A palace. Sometimes we'd opt to sleep in the houses with the rest of the band but mostly it was the back of the Dodge.

A kid from the Florida audience offered his floor for us to sleep on. We followed the kids with the truck and parked it in their driveway, the trailer sticking out and blocking the sidewalk. It was cool, it was cool, there were drunk kids everywhere, crawling onto the front lawn, in the bushes, leaving, just getting there, hanging in clumps. We were kind of supposed to keep things going, to be the entertainers. The guys from the band are the party guys. They expected it from us, we were exotic and a trophy of sorts. They gave us a place to sleep. Being charming was like rent.

The Florida kids looked familiar and akin to us as Californians. They all had blond hair and skateboarded. They were white and tan, in shorts and Vans, no different from the kids we'd grown up with. We started to nestle into corners of the living room and the kids started to leave, but then more would arrive. There was music and bongs and smoking and dirty furniture. The kids kept going, kept drinking and romping among themselves, and then as we started to doze, one of them opened their big Florida mouth and said something real racist. They all laughed. We were all spread out on the floor, draped over sofas, sitting up in chairs with our heads back. We looked at each other from our different points in the room. The realness of the difference between them and us became stringently apparent. Slowly. One by one, we got up and grabbed our stuff and ran from the house. We said nothing, got in our truck, and drove away. America was a cesspool.

We made a friend in the South named Chip, he was sexy and thick-boned. He wore a do-rag on his head and we helped him tar his roof. Chuck liked work that started early in the morning and earned a big lunch and a lot of weed. I got on his schedule. We became closer as we traveled. We'd get up early and I'd join his morning treasure hunt. If he couldn't find weed in pockets or in the carpet or around the apartment, he'd hit the street until he did. Chip put on the show in Mobile and Chuck met Pip, who he'd have two daughters with. At the show a skater got onstage and took a dog chain from his neck, leaned his head back, and lowered the end of it into his nostril. As the audience watched, he coughed the chain out of his throat so it went through his nose, then out of his mouth. He held each end of the chain by two hands, he'd done this before, and tugged it back and forth. That was his trick.

Our final show of the tour was in Phoenix and we all just wanted to go home. There was nowhere we needed to be and nothing we had to do, but we wanted to go home. We played our songs as fast as we could. Like we literally played them all as fast as we could as a joke and an homage to the end of the tour so we could just get out of there. We packed up fast, made a game of it, not talking to anyone and moving quick, like frantic robots, and drove.

21

·······

We got back to San Francisco broke and with no opportunity. For some reason we didn't unhook the trailer from the Dodge for a long time after we got back. We'd gotten good at parking with it and maneuvering it on the street. To roll it backward you needed to turn the steering in the opposite way you'd think. Like the tiller of a boat. I'd gotten good at it, Chuck had taught me. One day something happened on the freeway with it, though, and we pulled over in San Francisco traffic, unhitched the empty trailer, left it on the side of the road, and just drove away.

That was the mindset. Like a keyboard I'd had that I'd bought from Duane Hitchins, a composer in Los Angeles. He'd written songs from *Flashdance* on the keyboard and played the parts to "Da Ya Think I'm Sexy" by Rod Stewart. I bought it from him where he lived in the Hollywood Hills, following a want ad in the *Recycler*. I left that keyboard somewhere. In a studio in San Francisco that we shared with a band of women that we called the Lesbians. I just left it there without thinking about it and moved on. Actions like these surprise me now. I'm fully capable of not caring in that way, but it surprises me how easy it was then.

There was a record label from Los Angeles that

seemed interested in taking us on as a band and releasing our records, yet it didn't seem real and didn't change the fact that we all had no money. I started to work as a bike messenger. Mike Bordin went back to his job as a baker; I don't remember Billy working ever, but I got on a bike.

Bicycle messengering was unique in San Francisco, mostly because of the hills. Other cities had bike messengers but we had it tough with the hills. There was a language we had among ourselves, a talk and looks and a method. We were pirates out on the road, mostly punk rockers, shouting at each other on our walkie-talkies as we pedaled and delivered our packages. We'd meet at the Wall, a long, waist-high concrete shelf that stretched for a block. We'd taken it over in the middle of the financial district, downtown. The city made room for us. We'd sit at the Wall on our bikes and smoke and skateboard and pick on the businessmen. We hated the establishment naturally but there was pride in their attitude toward us. We'd ride through the streets and stop in clusters with friends and get high in alleys.

Some of us, like MaryJo, were really good at it. I wasn't. After I'd been promoted to a scooter, I took it home at lunch and sat too long watching TV and smoking pot, and some of the neighbor kids stole it. I got fired. It wasn't so much the loss of the scooter but the film negatives I'd had in my back basket that were part of a delivery. That was the rule. I was supposed to carry the deliveries with me when I got off the scooter to avoid the risk of them getting stolen. I never did, I always left them in the basket.

Things were real hand-to-mouth after that. I got a job in a movie theater down the street from my house called the York. It was a palace, unrivaled in its beauty, intact, and similar to the Strand in the movies it would show, but not as reckless. Already the face of San Francisco was changing. Slow like old age. Perceptible more now when I can look back at it.

To make money we'd heard of a drug-test study. Billy, Will, our friend Craig, and I stumbled onto it. There had been a sign on a telephone pole, the kind with the phone number hanging in perforated flaps that you could rip off and pocket. None had been taken. I tore the number off and brought it home and we called them on the phone. The premise was that we'd go into a room in a hospital from a Sunday through a Tuesday and be test studies for a drug that a company was developing. We'd be paid $225 and we'd sleep there and be fed. It was a lot of money to us. The study was being administered by a medical center above the Haight. The drug was called Ethmozine and we were told it was being developed to control heart rate. I made myself remember that word. Ethmozine. It doesn't come up later in the narrative, I just still remember the word.

The four of us packed extra clothes in knapsacks or bags that we brought with us on the Sunday evening and were checked in by the staff. We were treating it a little bit like a hotel, a home away from home, kind of a vacation. After checking in we were assigned to a room full of cots where we were to sleep, like an orphanage. The administration was strict and direct. There was lights-out and a breakfast in the morning before we'd get medicine'd.

"We want you all to be up and attentive after you've been administered the doses," the woman in the study instructed us. She was in street clothes with clean white tennis shoes and a baseball cap and a lanyard around her neck. We called her Coach behind her back. "You can watch television and sit in the chairs after the medicine, but you can't lie down or go to sleep. We need all of you up and attentive so we can monitor."

We understood. Our beds would be folded up into the walls after breakfast. We quickly reached a point of comradery with the other patients and were calling ourselves rats. Two twin brothers were in the study and a tall loner we called Pineapple Head. All of us, we were test rats and made a game of it. We made rat faces and flared our fingers like whiskers from our undernoses, rodents. We were upbeat and excited about the prospect of the effects of the drug. They gave it to us intravenously and we waited and watched each other.

Someone got dizzy. One of us threw up, someone started to cry. It wasn't good.

Coach panicked: "Bring down the beds!"

The beds came down from the walls and the crew in their scrubs scrambled nervously, quietly, pretending they knew what was happening. We all got back in the beds and rode the drug out. It wasn't so bad, some hot flashes and rumbling stomachs and fever. You'd think we'd have been skeptical when they announced they'd have to start the study over again because of the mishap, but it meant another weekend of work for all of us. That seemed good.

We worked the drug study and being in the hospital to our advantage. We returned the following weekend and did it all again, the overnight, the beds, the doses. We ordered horror movies into the ward that we'd watch to coordinate with the drug kicking in. *Texas Chainsaw Massacre* and *Nosferatu*. The doses were altered and no one got sick. After hours when the nurses went home and we were left on our own, we roamed the hospital halls and got in trouble. We stole boxes of syringes that we sold later to friends on the outside who shot drugs.

Making money was something new to most of us. Some of us had been doing it for a long time. I hadn't and it was a challenge. We developed scams. One involved flying. You'd check a bag at the airport and rip the tag off it at the luggage carousel when you landed. The bag needed to be small enough that it could double as a carry-on. You'd put that bag over your shoulder and take your original claim ticket to the lost-and-found window and report your bag missing. You'd describe the bag as being different and bigger than the one you'd put around your shoulder. After a back and forth the airline would apologize and promise a call later when they found the bag and you'd leave. Days later you'd receive a letter in the mail and a form to fill out. On it you'd list the things that were in the bag that had been lost, lying, exaggerating. Eventually, some weeks later, a check from the airline would arrive.

San Francisco was affordable and we took care of each other. We'd lived mostly like that, piecing meals together and sharing overages with friends and family. It was easy and doable but also just as easy to be on the road getting ten dollars a day.

I moved into a studio apartment with Jim Olson. It was a tiny and cheap studio on Nob Hill, right above the Tenderloin. Kimball Alley. The apartment had belonged to Matthew and somehow got passed down to Jim. It was dark, away from any sunlight, at the end of an alley. Big enough only for a bed and for some reason a bench and a rack with weights. The kitchen folded itself up behind two bending doors but it was tiny and barely used. We drank there with friends and screamed and wrestled at night until the landlord next door would bang and we'd stop for a while but always start again.

We would hear the cable car lines from the apartment, clanking and rattling. Cable cars ran on a system underneath the street. No engines or motors. The power source was centralized in the cable car barn and powerhouse at Washington and Mason streets. The cable looped nonstop; the drivers would clamp onto the line and the cars would be tugged along the tracks. The noise of this would come up through a slot in the middle of the street. I'd tell friends who visited that a tourist girl from the Midwest had stopped right there, on my corner, and went down on one knee to tie her shoe; her hair fell down into the slot and quickly wrapped around the cable and she was dragged for three blocks.

I told my father that story when he came and visited us in the apartment once on a business trip. He laughed and laughed at my story and didn't say anything about the one bed. We ate dinner and we ran for a cable car after. I remember him sprinting down Hyde Street in his suit and wing tips. His comb-over flopped wildly the wrong way, his glasses tipped askew. For some reason Jim and I were already on the cable car and he had to catch up. I cheered him on and was proud, seeing him sprinting in his suit. I'd seen him in roller skates in that suit.

Courtney came and stayed with us in that apartment on Nob Hill when we thought we could record music with a computer. It was too early in the trajectory of the technology but we were thinking it was possible. She came up in a huff and Jim eventually made her crazy and she retired to the shower and used a whole bottle of fancy hair conditioner that Rozy had given me. Courtney had caught wind that it was expensive. She ended up changing her flight and leaving early.

A space is neutral until it's turned into something. The studio we lived in was simply four walls. As our lives changed, it morphed into something energetic and magic. A place in which to sleep, to fuck, to worry, and to do drugs. Like a theater that's hosted a million performances, tragedies, comedies, musicals, flops, and standing ovations. The studio on Nob Hill, the physical space of it, was neutral until we started doing drugs in it. The hours spent waiting for the man changed our relationship with it. For a minute it was funny to hear that song playing as we waited. Then it wasn't. Things became less funny in general. She was always later than she said she'd be. The man. We'd hear her motorcycle at the top of the alley and listen as it puttered to a stop, then we'd hear a kickstand and the pushing of our big wooden gate that went to the stairs to the studio. It didn't matter, the lateness, at first. Later we'd be sick and wouldn't be better till we'd get high so the lateness became a big deal.

In the midst of a blossoming drug habit was our connection to each other in that space. Love is love is love. It happens like a steamroller and has no concessions for obstacles. In prison there's love. In the classroom there's love and also in the workplace. In offices and kitchens, in assembly lines, on construction sites. It happens where it's not allowed and it happens where it's encouraged. In times of complacency, in times of need, in times of duress, unexpectedly and often when you see it coming from so far away. There's no denying it when it happens. Jim and I were in love in the throes of growing up, in the mix of a drug habit, in a secret place where no one knew that it was.

22
. . . .

The band had earned a window of respect. We'd proved ourselves and had done a tour. Chuck had become a sort of Muppet celebrity in the village. Because he hated San Francisco he still only came up for shows. We started a back and forth between San Francisco and Los Angeles. San Francisco hated Los Angeles and Los Angeles was like, "Who's San Francisco?"

Things shifted when a record label in Los Angeles got serious. It was a label that had put out records by X. They were the first punk rock band I'd seen when I was in high school. The first record they had put out was by the Germs. That achievement alone was indisputable, an untouchable legacy. Slash, the label, was housed in an old Spanish wraparound two-story building on the corner of Beverly Boulevard and Hauser. There was a restaurant next door that had been sitting empty for dozens of years. One night, the restaurant just locked their doors, the tables set and ready. It never opened again and no one knew why.

Bob Biggs, who ran the company, was like an overgrown enthusiastic college kid, a golden retriever. He was goofy with thick glasses and an artist. He argued for symmetry but was crooked in an amiable way. He had a huge white standard poodle named Showbiz. His girlfriend,

Stella, was Greek and told me about the time she had sex with Joan Jett.

There is a world of music lovers, I'll always appreciate that. I'm one of them and it's a good place to be, among those who love it. I recognize people like me immediately. Slash was that place. The friends I met there treated what we did seriously. Randy Kaye, who worked there in a downstairs office, wasn't liked by the rest of the company. He was honestly really bitter and a challenge to be friends with, so I naturally was drawn to him and we became close until he passed. He looked kind of unhealthy and wore drab shades of beige and brown that did him no favors. His hair was thinning but consisted of one huge dreadlock that stretched down to the middle of his back. He had impeccable taste in music, like the best. He taught me so many things. Galaxy 500. Field Trip. He'd put out the first Spacemen 3 record and I loved him for that.

The band set about making a record with a different set of priorities. To be aware of sounds and tones and placements of frequencies, how they played in our mix, it was something we'd taught ourselves. We approached the process confidently, always knowing best, never compromising or giving in. There was a basketball hoop and ball we ignored, a pool table in a lounge that we left alone.

Chuck was a lot of work all the time. He had constant grievances and needs, and while the others laughed at him, I'd listen. I was sympathetic and a friend but it was tough to get behind something I honestly never felt appreciative of. Once in a while his lyrics would strike me as interesting or his singing would reach a weird tone that I could relate to. But so much work. It was challenging. He'd show up when it was time to sing and he'd have a cold. He'd smoke crack or angel dust on a bender, stay up all night, and come in to sing. His vocals were hobbled together with such thin thread, it never felt like it was gonna hold up. I didn't really believe in him but I never stopped rooting for him.

Live and onstage things were different. He was a mess and a shambles but his energy and charisma took over the rooms. I loved his laugh and his willingness. He'd wear makeup and dresses and wigs and clown shoes. A loud plaid with polka dots and some taffeta wrapped around a tutu. I don't know. We drove into Canada for a show after finishing the record and they wouldn't let Chuck in because of a drunk-driving arrest. Things like that would come up, surprises, things we hadn't known. His past would reveal itself in accidental ways. I tried to just be there, I like to think I understood secrets. The band turned on him and made him prove so much. It was really hard for him to deliver amid the strict expectations. We went into Vancouver without him; the rest of us sang his parts and screamed from the stage.

We finished a second record and played a show at Club Lingerie in Los Angeles to celebrate it. When I was young, it was really hard to get into a specific night there at that club. There was a dress-up night around the time that New Romanticism was edging its way into the punk rock circles. Steve Strange had hosted a night there after doing a record signing at Vinyl Fetish, the record store on Melrose run by two cranky older dandies. One of them was the father of Amra, who became one of my best friends. I took a record from the shelf that afternoon in the record shop, peeled the cellophane off it, and brought it up to Steve Strange for him to sign. I didn't pay for it.

It was the first Visage record and he winked at me suggestively. That night I tried to get into the Club Lingerie but
couldn't.

The arena of punk rock was only ever a boys' club.
What had started as a communal free-for-all, boys and
girls mashing against each other in the spirit of the loudness and the passion for the spirit of expression, changed.
Tough skinheads from suburbs came into Hollywood and
started to claim the dance floor for themselves. Things
got ugly. Girls weren't encouraged and fey boys got hurt.
Boots stomped and spikes poked and skanking turned
more physical than it had been. I couldn't have anything
to do with it. I was more scared than political; the moti-
vations were similar, one fed the other.

A chapter of prettiness came from England in the form
of the New Romantics and it was appealing, the dress-up
aspect, the dandyness. Adam and the Ants came to Hollywood and the boys from Huntington Beach arrived and
stuck stickers everywhere citing *BLACK FLAG KILLS
ANTS ON CONTACT.* That was how threatening the
look of pretty was to the tough boys. There was no question which side I was on.

Years later, our record release at Club Lingerie was
still special for me but also for the rest of the band. It was
a proud moment for us. Our record company came and
people who wanted to manage us came and my sisters
were there and friends from other bands and people who
wanted to write about us and learn more. It was all of
those who'd missed us before on the first go-round or had
seen us and still loved us. We played the show to a bigger
audience than we ever had and Chuck fell asleep onstage.
He lay down and went to sleep for a couple of songs. He

was drunk and tired and just didn't care. I've never seen anything like it. It was preposterous, ridiculous, unorthodox, and insulting, I loved it. A lot of people hated the show; that was also when Billy started talking about an ulcer.

23

·········

Who I was and what I stood for was a tug-of-war. A tug and a war. A combat between what I knew I should stand for and what I settled on. It's a waste of energy at that age to settle on anything. The thrive and the drive and the friction of what moved me was intense and at a peak that comes back infrequently. If I was reliving it or casting myself in a movie of it, I would go big. I would correct myself and aim for different stars. The stars in my sky at the time didn't twinkle or even shine, they were just close and reachable and I settled. Shame on me. There was shame on me. I was soaking in shame, in an easy and flexible manner, a tub of mud, an elixir of waste that served nothing, no one. The choices in my life were easy and driven by crowds or popularity or quick common reward. I didn't want to be gay.

We went on a tour with the sporty funky boy band that were popular at the time. Theirs was a real man energy, not too different from sports or heavy metal. You hear stories of straight boys in a circle jerk and wonder how that can happen, like does that really exist? It felt like that. They were dynamic and brotherly and really well liked. They were also sweet to us. I liked the bass player who was named after a bug. They did the tour in a bus and we, as the openers do, did the tour in a big Ryder box truck. We'd built a plywood wall in the back of it that separated the front seat from the rest of the truck. We made a sort of living space in the back. There was a sofa from our friend Joe's apartment. It was brown and of an old-lady fabric that stuck to your skin when it was moist. It was summer and things were wet, unbearably hot. Most of us would ride in the back of the hot Ryder, together on the sofa, with two of us up front, driving and navigating. We attached a tiny electrical fan to the cigarette lighter in the dashboard and positioned it at the top of the gap of the opening, directing the air-conditioning up into it so the cool would get to those in the back. We'd all huddle around it for the flow of the air. If you got too close your hair would get caught up in the fan, yanking it and stopping the blades. We'd all laugh. It happened to each of us only once, then we learned.

We met a crew of new people, and the ones from before all came and met us at the shows. Most of the kids were there for the headliner and wanted to get close to them. Chuck and I learned that quickly, they wanted to meet the singer, the other singer, and would pretend to like us to get close to them. We honestly weren't that likable. We were a musical tantrum, loud and pummeling. Sometimes in our shows we'd play the theme from the Nestlé white chocolate ad or an ad about the best a man could get, a razor made by Gillette. These would be the things people would talk about. That and "We Care a Lot."

I'd shaved off my dreadlocks; my head was bald and I'd taken to wearing red Dr. Martens, black spectacle frames, and a big white paper suit. It sweat too much on-stage but I thought the presentation was stunning. Joe and Chuck and I shouldn't have been, but we were smoking weed in front of some sort of frat house with a big lawn that we'd played at in Florida. The streets were crowded with big-haired girls and tan boys and we were who we were, smoking weed in the front seat of a big Ryder truck. A bald guy in a white paper suit and Chuck in some assemblage of fishnets and rips and Joe who had dreadlocks and looked like he'd just left a brawl. We got arrested and taken to jail. There is nothing like being in handcuffs, nothing. It is as real and literal as a word on a page, a bird in your hand, salt on the tongue. There is no arguing the immediacy of the situation and no regret or good intention can fix it. We were popular at the holding tank, first with the cops and then with the inmates. They hated us and laughed at our story, making fun of us. After spending the night in the cell, the rest of the band came and bailed us out and we drove to the next city.

It was all really stressful for Billy. He took the valleys personally, personal affronts on himself. There was a lot of talk about his ulcer and how the disrespectful episodes we'd get into as a band were killing him. I'd shut up when he said that and imagine his stomach rotting and burning. I understood it was mostly Chuck, but I knew it was also me who made him crazy. His was a complicated set of balls to juggle. His sense of musical drama and melody and tension was so unique and astute. It could have stopped there but he had that inherent need to take on the responsibilities of our well being, the business and administration of what had to be done. Without his passion we wouldn't have moved forward, straight up. He kept his eye on our agenda, things the rest of us ignored, and we all benefited from it. I didn't care enough to take things beyond the then and present.

24
········

We traveled as a band to Europe. The logistics of making that happen were insanity. Luggage and equipment and travel and places to stay. The computer had barely been invented and everything was done by phones. We had illegal credit card numbers that we'd use for long-distance calls. I don't know where the numbers came from, we'd share them with friends and other bands and call home with them, talking for hours on pay phones. We learned lots of tricks to cut corners. We invented tricks.

England was cold and wet and the color of fingernails. The food was horrible and we navigated ways to survive, ways we hadn't. It was a struggle. We learned Indian food. We were surrounded by exotic things that we embraced. An Englishman showed me his boils, spread his ass cheeks. He worked with us. I'd never seen that. It seemed like an English condition. There was an appreciation for what we were that surprised me, constantly.

When we first arrived, the slogan *WE CARE A LOT* was everywhere. The biggest posters I'd ever seen. Chuck and his dreadlocks, the mishmash of the rest of us flocking him. I wondered if the record company had plastered specific walls between the airport and our hotel so we'd see them and be impressed. We were never not skeptical.

Badges and patches and promotional shirts. Courtney had told me that cracking the UK was easy. Like she knew. But yeah. It's a small island and there were just two publications that covered absolutely everything in the world of music. Everyone on that island followed music, even grandparents. I loved that. They all watched *Top of the Pops*.

We stayed at the Columbia Hotel and it was a messy and glamorous time. We'd all been up and traveling and jet-lagged. Jim, the guitar player, had hit Joe, Chuck's good friend who had come with us to help with guitars. They were both drunk and Jim's hand was broken and in a splint. Joe went home in a tantrum right away, flew right back to Los Angeles, and Jim did the tour with his broken hand. We did an interview with one of the big music publications in the lobby of the hotel that afternoon and fought our way through it. Our fighting among ourselves became an expectation and a calling card. A tangle of arguments and proud standoffs among us. Sonically and representationally, we argued and fought in public. The English applauded our dysfunction, they were fascinated with American trash.

There was a crew of kids we immediately met in London. Andy, Karen, Kerry, Clemencey, Ruth, Mole, Linda, Martina. They followed us as we toured up through the UK and back down to London. They would hitchhike or take cheap trains and sleep in petrol stations. I'm still friends with most of them, they supported us from the start. We would put them on our guest lists and bring them food from the backstage and give them floor space to sleep on in our hotels. They were scrappy and young and they all carried knapsacks or backpacks or rucksacks. They called them their kits.

There was a drunken despondency to Chuck and his performance. Billy, more than any of us, couldn't deal with it. It was a befuddled neglect, a sloppy and disrespectful show of nonchalance, a slap in the face to the progress we'd made. It was always funny to me, but funny is so subjective. Drunk and belligerent onstage was a really hard stance to get behind. The craft of what the three of us had created, me and Mike and Billy, it was cheapened when Chuck was drunk. He'd push it as far as he could and then get accolades for his performance. It depended who you'd talk to. There were fans and there were criticisms. Among the band we became more and more critical until I was outvoted.

I forced myself to cry when we fired him. Back in San Francisco, I was in a car listening to a cassette of him playing acoustic guitar and I was squeezing my eyes really tight to make the tears come. I told myself I was going to start a new band and call it Chuck. There was a nostalgia and a loyalty that I let myself get swept up in. I felt genuinely moved. And then not. I honestly hadn't believed in what we'd accomplished, the records, the shows, all of it, but I loved Chuck. He'd become a big part of my life but the band was weighty, like an old established relationship, and I clung to it.

Change is lonely. Progress is tedious, steps are so small. The streets in San Francisco winter are slick and slippery. It's cold and everything is washed out and if you don't cross the wet streetcar tracks at a perpendicular angle, the wheels of a bike can come out from under you. Jim Olson taught me that. I'd fallen lots on my motorcycle and it was hard to pick up the heavy bike after I'd gone down. It was a time I was strong and convicted, charming and late to things, well dressed and generous. I wasn't judgmental, I was critical and challenging and wanted outrageous outcomes and unpredictable times. I loved pushing things too far and wanted company as I did it.

What is love when you don't want it? When you're scared of it and need to keep it under wraps? What is gay when you don't want to be? The tedium of not knowing who I was took a toll. Is that what happened? Hiding, like in a game as a child, and not being found is a victory. What if the hiding place is so good that you're never found? At first it's such a triumph that no one can find you. And then . . . what if the hiding place is dark and dank and hard to breathe in and you discover the lid of the box you're hiding in locks from the outside? The panic. The horror. Being hidden was what I thought I wanted.

In the studio apartment above the Tenderloin we continued to use drugs. It started so casually, simply another flavor of distraction to what was really going on. We'd fuck and love each other in the dark. It was apparent from the start that we'd keep it hidden to protect ourselves. The drugs and the love. They were connected.

Our best friends were Lynn and Helen. Jim, Lynn, Helen, and me. The four of us would go out and get drunk and pummel each other. It was like an extension of the mosh pit that I'd never participated in. We would tackle each other and hurt ourselves and scream and laugh and do it again and again. We'd go way too far every time and someone would end up angry and storm off while the rest of us ate late diner food till we got sick.

Lynn and Helen had been in a band together called the Wrecks with Jone and Bessie when they were teenagers in Reno. They famously broke up onstage in Canada opening up for Black Flag when Helen, the lead singer, froze and couldn't perform. They had lived in the Haight when Lynn was playing drums with the Dicks. I met Lynn and Helen through Jim. He and I would sometimes sleep in their closet. The four of us would go on adventures. We drove to Nevada and camped in the desert and swam naked in the Hoover Dam. We ended up in Laughlin and stayed with Helen's father, an alcoholic who worked in a casino. San Francisco remained pleasantly aimless. Friends with higher ambition would move away.

25
....

Courtney had moved to Los Angeles. It was an unbelievable coup and feat that she'd gotten a full-page profile in *Interview*. There was a similar profile in the same issue of Kevin Hunter, a singer from San Francisco who'd been in a punk rock band with ambition called Wire Train. We were jealous of him and at the bottom of his page was the word *ADVERTISEMENT*. Oh, Courtney loved that. When I took her to the airport in the middle of a fight, she was stopped by the airline for not having an ID. She rolled her eyes and marched over to the magazine stand and grabbed the *Interview* off the rack, brought it back to the check-in counter, and opened it up to the page with her face, punching it with her finger as proof of who she was.

She was on her way to South America somewhere to be in a movie with Joe Strummer and the man from the Pogues and Elvis Costello. Courtney's role was a pregnant woman and she didn't like the way she looked on-screen with her stuffed stomach in the rushes she'd seen. She told me on the phone that she'd started moving the stuffing out of her costume to look slimmer. This was her becoming famous on her own terms.

Without Chuck, the band didn't have a lead singer. We

talked it to death, the prospects. Mike and Jim had met Mike P in Eureka when we'd played there on tour and they reached out to him. He was really young and in another band. His voice was incredible and undeniable, he could emulate anything. Popular singers at the time. Sade, Axl Rose, George Michael. We had written a bunch of songs and Mike came to San Francisco and sang on them as sort of an audition. It was really different to have that kind of finesse over the songs we'd created. The melody lines and the performances he pulled off were above and beyond anything we'd expected.

A glaring element in the mix that had been neglected and specifically ignored was where a voice can take the songs. We'd put so much creed into the execution of the music, of what we'd done as musicians. It was a beautiful foundation but everything hinged on what a singer would do. Mike changed everything.

We made a record with the finished songs. Mike P was committed but also resistant. He didn't want it and he did. The record we made together was a new beginning. There were flavors and a steady consistency in the volatile mix of the songs that we made that we hadn't had before. We played a show at the IBeam in San Francisco and Mike cut his hand open on a bottle on the edge of the stage. There were stitches, it was really bad, there was talk of losing feeling in his hand. It wasn't a good start. He resented the situation for what it was. It was an opportunity with a really high price tag, more dangerous than promising.

Mike P didn't drink or smoke. He wore bicycle shorts with a fanny pack, he had long hair, and his baseball cap was backward but off-center. He was a jock but a poet, his dad was a coach. He had a brother who became a policeman. He was a lot younger than the rest of us and came from a completely different place. He was really physically fit and he loved Arsenio Hall and Sade. In San Francisco I drove him around on the back of my motorcycle, trying to figure him out. I was helping him track down Sade after her concert there. I was humoring him. He was certain that finding her was an option, like a kid who keeps hoping for something that's clearly not gonna happen. I let myself get caught up in it with him. We were sure we'd see her in the mix of the hotels in Union Square.

San Francisco was changing but remained unhinged and unbridled, the limp that it staggered on had shifted but the wobbly walk was the same. Billy had moved into an abandoned pet hospital on Fell Street near Market. It was a truly phenomenal geographic that could only exist then, not now. There was an outside roof area upstairs where we'd smoke and drink and it was lined with huge, rusted cages and a stench of old animals that never went away. There were operating tables on wheels and ancient surgical equipment where carcasses had been worked on. Billy had established his own friend group that I wasn't a part of. There was no changing the fact that we'd spend the time together we'd need to, to keep the band going. Anything more than that seemed redundant and we developed lives apart from each other.

The same with Mike Bordin, who lived with his girlfriend, Merilee, near where I lived with my boyfriend, Jim. When Mike P made the decision to make a record with us, he moved in with Mike and Merilee. He was nineteen or twenty and we had no money to pay him. I made some money working movie theaters still and sometimes

I'd type fast in big office spaces for companies that paid me well. We all were living different lives. I had my own.

There was a real resistance to a new singer from the friends who used to like us. We had cut Chuck loose and it seemed coldhearted to a lot of our world. We'd traded him out for someone younger, more sexy, and white. Our choice looked ugly and safe to some, geared toward broader strokes. I'd always considered our decisions to be artful and unorthodox, an undercurrent of surprises and fucked-up twists with a disregard for conventional results. I didn't understand what it meant or how it happened, but as we moved forward with new songs, I heard us regarded as a rock band. The direction with Mike P took its own course.

In our pursuit we'd progressed and moved forward, and with that progression a gate had opened. We went through the gate and it swung and hit me as I passed, and forever more I hear it as it clangs against itself behind me. We'd moved on. A band is a democracy and one thing I do well is work with others. It comes from a place of growing up. Being in the middle of a mix of four children, there had been a constant need to smooth things over. I like to make things right. At some point, though, even if things were right, I got addicted to problems, things being broken enough for me to be able to fix them and in turn be rewarded. In our old house on Plymouth, it was a trick of mine to hide my mother's purse to create the drama of something lost, especially when she was late and in a frantic sort of rush. I'd let the situation stew and then present the purse, as if I'd found it, and be the hero.

I craft words in my head. When I'm not talking and staring into space it's what I'm doing. I love the way letters work together. The song and the nuance of a lilted vowel, a swooping double-l into an o sound, the meaning and entendre of a hinted suggestion, the bite of a lyrical twist, when a passage turns unexpectedly, the nuance of a passive aggression, all of it fascinates me. It's odd that I didn't pay attention to what Mike P was singing about at the time we went into the studio and started recording. It was the last thing on my mind and that's unnerving to look back on. It wasn't until real recently that I sat down with Mike's lyrics and had a payoff with the craft of what he'd created.

In this first record we all made together, he was young and naive and strong-willed and confident. His talent was refined and studied. I noticed mostly that he'd taken on roles or characters or personas in his writing. He'd be a baby in one song, an old man in another. It was hard to decipher who he was and I couldn't figure him out. His voice did a similar trick. It wasn't consistently any one thing. He was taking cues from the rest of us, we were doing the same thing. We weren't sticking to any one particular style of music or song or theme. Being slippery and elusive felt like an advantage and a showing-off of sorts, like a look at what we can do. Personally, the duality and the disparity of who I was and how I lived was acting out.

There was a darkness in the sun that was Los Angeles when we'd go back there. There is shit through the smile that's LA. It was like spotting an old and dear friend from really far away, and as you approach, their hair is thin and wrong, made of bugs, their eyes brown socket holes and their mouth a mess of rotted corn teeth. You can be friends still, it's just that the smell is so bad.

We played a show with our new singer at the Roxy on

Sunset Boulevard and it was peppered with people who suddenly loved us, people we didn't know. How Slash and the other one from the Guns and the Roses ended up onstage with us is beyond me. Courtney was such a grubby fame whore, we both were. She was cackling and excited and I went there with her. We grabbed at each other in a crowded hallway as I came offstage after the encore because it was something, it was attention, it was drama. It had been arranged, though, like a marriage we hadn't asked for. A manager who'd started to work with us had ties to that world of dress-up, campy rock music in Los Angeles, and it was a favor to him, those famous rock people joining us onstage. To the world's credit, though, those musicians liked us, they were applauding what we were doing, and I can't complain or act like a spoiled child in the scenario. It's a funny thing about flattery, it doesn't ever matter where it comes from, it will always make me feel.

After the Roxy we went next door to the Rainbow Room. I'd never been there; it was where Lemmy of Motörhead hung out on off nights. We'd spent time as children on the Sunset Strip but only ironically, sarcastically, tempting the fate of police as we smoked and drank small bottles of whatever from bags on curbs in front of punk rock. We were scrappy, not the leathered slick rock monsters who ended up staking claim. Not like that at all, but sort of akin to the Manson girls who crawled from the Strip to downtown in a desperate attempt to get attention. We were out of place in the club and we spat on the carpet that was being rolled out for us. On the dance floor we found Milli Vanilli, the two performers from Germany who girl-you-know-it's-true'd their way into our hearts

on the MTV. We were beyond ourselves and we danced
with them and rollicked in the absurdity of what that
all was. Them on the crest of their voyage, before being
shunned and laughed at and pushed to a place of suicide.
Times like these shine absurdly, brightly, as beacons of
vague directions, points on a path that were dead-ending
somewhere.

26

....

W hat followed was a stretch of forever, an optimistic head-down and tunnel-visioned pursuit to nowhere, an era of never allowing ourselves to say no. There was no such thing as an edit, it was just yes to every opportunity that came our way.

Ours was a youthful and boundless energy, eager and blissful, never-ending sarcasm and bite and observation and wit. Being a performer, working in that realm meant never being off, always being on. We were watched, taken pictures of, written about, and applauded, I lived a life of show. It was a hilarious response from the world we'd asked for, it delivered its promise and we continued to feed it. The attention that came as we steamrolled forward was fueled by lots of things but led by a want of a pretty face and a palpable sound. It was unthinkable that we were suddenly that. Mike P was a beautiful kid, and no matter how we tried to downplay or contrast that beauty with shit, he shined. The songs did a similar trick, where they might have been inside jokes or twists or statements of depravity from our innards, they hit, they were hard, and they had kids' heads banging up and down in a surprisingly traditional way.

We kept at it relentlessly and toured in different iterations. The company we were keeping, the bands we played with, usually felt like distant cousins, not entirely like us, but not really that different either. There was a distinct drive among us as bands. Some didn't care and I'd be jealous and appreciative of those ones. There was a narrative and a thread there that was so odd. Decisions kept being made for us and we were surprisingly complacent in acceptance. We always said yes. It was usually just easier.

New York City was a merry-go-round of taxis to photo shoots and interviews. The montage of it swirls and jolts in muted colors, pops of taxi yellow, cityscape brown, rain and dripping overhangs, bowls of dirty candies in backstages that overcompensate, office buildings even, elevators and coffees from the street, faces and faces and faces, it happens so fast. There was a strong and relentlessly intelligent woman named Kim, I can see her arm upraised calling the millionth cab for us, focused and determined to get us somewhere, another interview, another photo shoot, while we untangled out onto the buzzing streets on an impossible schedule. There was a sudden willingness to listen to what we had to say. Given the opportunity to be heard, we spoke of things we shouldn't and let it be known we weren't stupid rockers. We had things to say and continued to separate ourselves from the traditional stances that other bands took.

Photographers started to ask Mike P to come forward in the photo and we'd shoot them down. There was a guarded and prideful sense of protection that accompanied our quest for success, so inherent in all of us. We continued to be hard on ourselves, watching each other like hawks in those scenarios. How dare anyone ask for anything or take on a role of assumption or reap the benefits of what we'd worked for. We were really uptight in our vigilance. Like new mothers, protective of their first kids. Mad at them too. Enough to leave and get drunk behind closed doors.

Major moments came and went. There was a room with a bathtub in the compound that was *Top of the Pops*. We'd do that show in London and do it again and again, and I'd go back to that room upstairs in the dressing rooms. The English were so accommodating. It was through a maze of backstage and the tub was old and clawfoot, oversized. We'd be at the studio all day from an early start and I'd lie in the tub and add hot water for hours with my Walkman headphones on. My skin was red and heated, still steaming, and I'd explore the circus of that world and eat scones and clotted cream in the studio café. I saw a Radiohead in the bathroom and asked him if their band hated each other.

"Absolutely not," he let me know.

Noted, Radiohead.

My band was taking pride in our disdain for each other at that point, we'd resigned to exist as rivaling siblings, we would push that. The eccentricities among us that didn't meld and couldn't work.

From *Top of the Pops* back to ugly America and back to *Top of the Pops*. It was an assault of adoration and ambivalence. Back and forth. Courtney had been right, the UK was an easy victory, so simply conquerable. It's a tiny country and applauded our bad behavior, our irreverence, Americanisms that were gross to us and other Americans. We had become something there, our people, our audience was more open-minded, had more hair, wore leather jackets. They weren't as odd as they'd been before and this I noted. The differences happened slowly and I adjusted to make room for better meals, more affordability, bigger audiences.

We always stayed at the Columbia Hotel in London when we could afford better. The key chains for the rooms were massive, big knockers of brass too big for a pocket. We gave them back to the receptionist as we'd leave the hotel for the day and they'd hang the keys on hooks behind the front desk. I met an actress named Olivia who I'd meet again years later in rehab. She reached over the desk and stole a key from a hook as I distracted the receptionist and she and I stayed in that room for a week. There were feathers and hats and heels and rolling suitcases and cigarettes and big pints of beer in a bar that never closed. There was hash sprinkled into rolled tobacco, there were cans of ale that we'd poke holes in to smoke through, there was foil we'd ask the front desk for.

In Berlin we performed on a night at the Loft and someone shouted in an ear between the end of our set and the encore that the wall had come down. While we were onstage the Berlin Wall had come down. I remember announcing that from the microphone onstage, not knowing anything of anything and being a truly naive American idiot. The strength and magnitude of what had gone down became apparent as we drove out of the city to travel to our next show in Oslo. The traffic stopped and Germans were out of their cars drinking champagne and celebrating in the streets. Dense crowds of strangers were crying and hugging each other in the night. East Germans were streaming into West Berlin. History had changed in a night. We couldn't stay and revel in the change, we had somewhere to be and we left.

As the tour winded down the band became popular.

Very popular. It was roughly eighteen months of constant moving and touring and performing that earned us fans and new people, but when we stopped, record sales really kicked off. It was hard to say no to things that came up, to opportunities and adventures. We as a band weren't necessarily answering the questions, things were being decided, and a tour with Robert Plant in smaller cities throughout America felt charming and we did it. It was a humble time. We went to pawnshops every day and I bought an accordion.

I'd been to a gay bar in a small town the night before on a day off. It was what I'd do before I discovered the ease of the one-stop of a sex club. Standing alone in a dark part of a gay bar, peeling the wet label off a beer with my fingernail and waiting. It took too long.

The next day we were out at thrift stores and pawnshops with Robert Plant, he was a sweet man. It was hot and he wanted a drink and suggested going to a bar off the street. We all agreed of course, and he chose unknowingly the gay bar I'd been in the night before. It was right there and there was no indication what it was, no sign, no rainbow flag. I could only say, "Sure," and we went in and they realized quickly what it was. It was cool with Robert and it was cool with us. We drank together in the small-town gay bar. Which sounds like no big deal but it really was to me at the time. We left the bar and a kid with a pickup truck offered us a ride to the hotel and we all got in the back and headed off. Us and Robert Plant.

Around that time, we opened up for Billy Idol for some months. I kept citing his old band Generation X in defense of us doing it. They felt mildly real, back before Billy Idol had become what he was. He'd come from some sort of legitimate background and was a small-town punker before he became a cartoon. To be clear, I loved the cartoon as well. He had a handler who had the demeanor of a man who'd just gotten out of comedy school. Ridiculous and extreme and gregariously scoring coke at any given twist of the day. There was an energy that dominated these big scenes of rock, an assumption of straightness. It wasn't our thing.

Aside from me being gay, it was too easy for everyone in the band to fall into that role. My base response was to back out and not take part. When songs with the band would come up that were overtly aggressive and didn't speak to me, I just wouldn't play on them. There were only a couple. One of the songs Jim wanted to make a music video to and chopped a chicken's head off in a parking lot. Like that's kind of it in a nutshell.

27

....

When we finally stopped touring, I was with my family for Christmas. I bought my mother an oversized bear, it was a gesture of grandeur that I couldn't afford. I'd saved per diems and had some hundreds of dollars in a plastic bag that I was proud of. I was so conditioned to making no money that the notion of it coming in wasn't feasible and didn't seem real. I was on the sidewalk and my father was on roller skates, two of my sisters were sitting on our front steps, and an envelope was delivered to me at my parents' home. It was a check from the band in the amount of over $12,000, my share of what we'd made over the past year and a half of touring. My father was so proud. I can remember the way he smelled and the rub of his shaved face on mine as he kissed me congratulations. I honestly had nothing to spend the money on.

I was still living in the studio apartment in San Francisco with Jim. We had been watching the stock market in the same way we watched the MTV. Because it was pro-establishment and what straight people did and a clearly not-cool thing to do among our peers. We obnoxiously exaggerated our leanings, bragging, talking companies and CEOs in front of artist friends performatively. Jim encouraged me to buy stock in Apple at the time because Steve Jobs was rumored to be coming back to the company and they were at an all-time low. I did exactly that and it changed my life. I took the check and bought stock in the company and I still have that stock. I sold a small piece of it to buy my apartment in New York City ten years ago, but I still have most of it. It's millions and millions of dollars. When I tell this story I like to insist how I'm not bragging, it's an accidental win, like winning a lottery. That's true and it's not. Blindly I knew exactly what I was doing.

Not to put a price tag on my relationships and the friends that I've chosen, but in terms of the big picture, money talks. Jim was ridiculous and belligerent, impossibly challenging and over-the-top, an intellectual bully. Most of my people couldn't stand him and I realize now he was possibly schizophrenic. It's a diagnosis Matthew shared with me when he spoke to Jim's brother, who'd been with him before he passed. His condition and who he was were insanity for anyone to put up with. As a boyfriend and a live-in partner it was unthinkably treacherous and complicated. The amount of grief and the navigating of a million different social scenarios in the course of our relationship made my coming out so much harder than it ever needed to be. If I could be honest about that relationship and who I was then, that's what it was to people, that's what being gay was. A spinning catalog of highs and lows above and below the tolerance level of any form of sanity. Me being gay was me making the choice to be with someone as maniacal as Jim. Me being gay was me making the choice to invest $12,000 in Apple that would eventually make me a millionaire. It's complicated.

The friends I made, the friends I make, particularly the prickly ones who other friends can't stand, I will do anything for. My loyalty is my strength and my pride and the place I rest assuredly, the place I know that's right. No one can touch this perspective, it's a constant sanction, a refuge of what I know to be right in the world. My friends and my lovers I respect and protect. I don't know how I came to be that way.

I continued to stand behind Courtney and I was always alone in my posturing. She would burn through friend after friend after friend but there weren't many of me. She had moved to Los Angeles full-time and thrown herself into a cusp of indie rock that was respectable and noisy and had a sense of royalty. Jeffrey Lee Pierce, Nick Cave, the Pixies, she was fueled by a world of noise in music that Kim Gordon could be named the queen of. She made a record that Kim produced and I saw Hole play one of their first live shows at the Coconut Teazer on Sunset Boulevard. Courtney screamed authentically, roared in a vivid way that laid bare the punch and realness of what she'd always been. She was made to scream that way, it was in her very soul to be on a stage and scream, to prolificate, to be looked at. She stayed too long on the stage. She always overstayed her welcome, she didn't need to play that long, but her performance and presentation were glorious, resonant, triumphant.

I borrowed my family's car and drove with Courtney and her drummer, Caroline, to Tijuana. My band was playing a show and Courtney was explaining why Caroline smelled the way she did. She wasn't wearing underwear. I couldn't smell what she was talking about and Courtney said it was because I was gay. We walked through the streets leading away from the border, the circus and hive of sales and shops and street sellers of plastic things, men, just men everywhere, and Courtney in her see-through slip with ballet flats and nothing else. She was screamed at by literally every man on the street, they wouldn't stop and she was oblivious. She reacted the same to the criticisms from my bandmates. They hated her and she pushed them further, got in their faces in a dramatic stance for effect.

In Los Angeles she and I would shoot drugs with Jennifer on the roof of a fucked-up Craftsman next to the 110. Four or five kids lived in the house, up on the roof was a hum from the freeway, not fifty feet away. I hadn't put a needle in my arm before, Jennifer did it for me that first time. Jennifer was young and in a band and hers is one of two or three phone numbers I can still recite from the 1980s. We were all on that rooftop together, high and nodding out, saying back and forth, "I don't feel it." That was always the general call for more. "I don't feel it."

If I'd felt that drug. If I could have acknowledged the high and the tableau of difference between straight and not, would I have been able to recognize the grade between happy and shit? There was a common battle cry among us that we didn't feel it. The need for more, the need for attention, the need for something to spearhead an emotion, it wasn't only mine. The want for it, the desire to push, to feel the push, to scratch an itch, to feel the itch, anything, my people and I, we ached. I wasn't alone. I was alone but I wasn't alone.

Courtney likened the drug to a wise old soothsayer woman, an inescapable lair. We were still dabbling with the drug and not strict or committed about it, but Jennifer was. She was studied and strong and got shit done. She'd developed a habit in a professional way, very Los Angeles. Courtney was still taking anything she could from anyone who'd entertain her and I continued to champion her finding herself while I looked for me.

In San Francisco we smoked the heroin on tinfoil. Once it started it was hard to turn off. We'd be at the beach on towels on a bright gray day and someone would bring it up like a joke. Sabotaging the sun and the perfection, we'd shit on it all and make a call to the woman on the motorcycle who would deliver. She'd use our apartment to skin-pop the drug into her leg. It was scary and bold and a doubling down of who I didn't dare to be. There was a sense of pride in doing something so wrong, and at the same time we kept the drugs really close to our chests and were secretive about it. No one should have to know that, the dark door we'd opened.

The weekends got longer, they stretched from Thursday until even Monday, late Monday, and my nose started to run when I stopped. I didn't see it coming, it smelled like the warning of waiting an hour after eating before swimming. I never believed a cramp would come or dopesick would happen to me. There was a rift between the success of what we'd achieved as a band and my mental health, the drug abuse.

My family had been my biggest champions. My father told me he now knew what to say when people asked about me. "He's a musician," he'd say. My sisters were behind me and always surprised and supportive of my antics. The heroin was too much. My sister Stephanie had come up to San Francisco to make sure everything was okay. It was but it honestly wasn't, and what we were doing behind closed doors became a thing. Friends had begun to notice and things were being said. It was jarring, getting high, getting sick, getting high, and getting sick.

It hurt too much and it felt too good and the rip-roar of the up-and-down of that trajectory tore everything apart. It hadn't started that way. At first we were just coasting through celebrations. Initially it was doable.

I don't know if it was the supermodels or Seattle, but *heroin chic* was a phrase. Courtney met Kurt and the face of the drug changed. As if it had hired a PR firm. There were users and scenes and references to people cooler than us who were strung out, but Kurt and Courtney changed it all and really put it on the map, becoming more like milk-carton kids than poster kids. I need to speak personally because clearly there were minions of fans and friends and followers who weren't obsessed in that way and didn't go that route. I was the type who was affected and did.

I was in a car going over the Bay Bridge with a sister when I first heard it. Anyone I know can remember where they were when it first happened. I knew it was out but hadn't yet heard it. The feel of that song for the first time was a wallop of profundity. Think of where you were. The tone of the music wasn't that different and felt relatable and familiar, a reckoning, a messy chaotic mélange. But the voice. The scream. I held my breath as I realized what it was. I was excited and scared and jealous and wanted to be close to it all at once. Courtney had prepared me, she knew better than anyone what was about to happen. She'd heard the new songs on the *Bleach* tour. She'd been at those shows and she knew. Her pursuit of Kurt wasn't about the success factor of those songs. To suggest as much is common and discredits her in an ugly, misogynistic way. Courtney has and retains an astute appreciation and obsession of craft and passion. She has always championed a specific method that's honed through darkness and learning, from a unique and lived-in space and history. She pursued Kurt because he was a genius of that craft.

I met him first at a show in Los Angeles at the Palace Theatre. She and I had arrived before they played, she had the only laminate and tugged me by my hand, stomping through it all up the stairs to their dressing room. She bombed their camp with her presence, I could feel it backstage as we passed people. They wouldn't make eye contact with her, but the second she passed their eyes would roll or they'd say something behind their hands to each other. I was a beat behind her and I watched it happen as we walked. Kurt loved that about her and I loved that about Kurt. He recognized her power, demonstrative, indisputable, and unrivaled. She'd been honing that force forever; she turned tables over just by walking in the room.

At her apartment in the foothills of Hollywood later, after the show, Kurt was shy and quiet and funny and odd. He was by himself in our small crowd and he sat on a greasy armchair next to a dead plant, neglected and unwatered. His smile was hesitant and naughty, sarcastic and wise. The show had been everything. The voice was everything. The presence, the growl, the ease and abandon, the power, it was absolutely heroic. It was such a loud noise, the three of them. The drums were so big, they did everything you wanted them to do. The sound and the furor fit so comfortably on us, familiar but fresh, soothing and jarring, challenging and new. But it was the voice. It was all about Kurt's voice. I overcompensated with him and talked too much. In the end I became friends with him by being quiet. And in the meantime, heroin was cool.

I made drug connections in different cities. In San Francisco there was the girl on a motorcycle who delivered. In Los Angeles there was Clare, an older goth woman who lived off of Hoover in an old Spanish apartment building that was light blue. It was embarrassing and cool to be seen there. Those who'd been doing the drug longer would hold their heads down if you passed them in the hallway to her apartment until you called them out and they'd look up surprised. I was young and new enough to not care if people knew I was buying dope.

There was a time when my band played a one-off in Tijuana, not the time when Courtney and Caroline came with me, another time when we flew. I arrived the day before the show and hadn't brought enough heroin to keep me good. I walked back over the border and found the band's big equipment truck parked at the airport in San Diego and drove it back to Los Angeles, to Clare's apartment, where I scored and immediately drove back to Mexico in the Southern California traffic. I stopped at a diner off the 5 headed south and asked for a spoon with my coffee and took it to the bathroom and shot up. I left the truck where it had been parked at the airport, and with the syringes and dope I walked back over the border, right through customs. After the show I was in a seat in the passenger van, up near the front, and a manager's wife who was Christian was there, and I told her about how I was a Catholic kid. I insinuated a little too passionately that my ties weren't that distant with the Lord. Heroin.

I'd get back to San Francisco on a plane and Jim

would mostly meet me at the airport with dope in the car. That was where we were with the habit, it happened fast. There's a word for it and I can't recall what it is, but I knew and I know now that when you stop the drug cold turkey and then start again later, there's no forgiveness. You are back to where you were the last time in your habit instantly. What's that word, it's such a cruel phenomenon. At the early stage of the habit I'd be restless when I didn't get high. My nose would run and my legs would kick at night. Not much more suffrage than that. And then it got so much worse.

The payoff of the high of the drug wasn't that perceptible at first. It's subtle and never what you want it to be. There's never enough, ever, and it's hard to acknowledge the effects. There's an inherent need and desire for more, that's part of it. At its best, it's a dimming of the lights to a comfortable level where talking and being with the world is sexy and personal and casual. There's a pall that's created that invites the ease to converse, to share things, to be a smoother version of yourself. The world is relatable and a sense of communion is thick and apparent, others want to connect with me as much as I do with them. Once that bliss is honed in on, going back to sober hurt. The edges and focus of being straight later, or two days later, are bright with too much exposure.

At first it was social. I'd share the experience with friends and even first-timers, looking for connections. Eventually it turned into a more lonely place. Jim and I would lie on the futon in the studio apartment and just pass that foil back and forth between us with a rolled-up hollowed-out pen for a straw. The brown drug would burn and smell like cotton candy. It hurt in the lungs and that might have been the tinfoil, the carcinogens. Immediately it soothed the tummy that ached for it.

Kurt was all about that for as long as I knew him. His tummy hurt. His ailments went beyond a need for the drug or a soothe to the sickness of not having it. He had stomach issues. It seemed all drug-related to me and a call for heroin to help. Through most of the times we spent together he was sick and needing drugs. There were scenarios and periods of ease and conversation and sharing, but we were always high. We both hated to eat. A meal was just something to get through to smoke a cigarette. We both ate ice cream and his was strawberry Häagen-Dazs. He loved that I was gay because he wanted to be. He loved the buttons that being gay pushed. Contrarily, he was also from a weird small town in Washington that didn't allow that and sometimes he seemed like an old man from there with fucked-up values. Heroin made him gayer and more complacent as far as I could tell.

In San Francisco the band had started writing and recording again. I was shoveling my way through the reactionary record and fell asleep on a sofa between the mixing board and the window into the control room in a studio. The day after getting too high was always blissful and sleepy. It was clear in the process of the studio and our new record that there was a lot to prove. The landscape out in the world we existed in had changed. The world and community of rock-loving children had changed partly because we'd changed it. There was an acceptability of clichés in old rock motifs that called out and wanted to be addressed in new ways. The Flying V guitar, a relic of an old-fashioned era, something we'd laughed at and scoffed, was freshly adapted and ironically accepted. Punk rock had been a lot about shaving away the hair that represented that past, and now that hair was chic and representative of a tongue and a cheek. There was an avenue and a place we were expected to go and it would have been an easy course to follow. We could have made it easy on ourselves and made a record that was digestible and palpable. The idea of becoming the band that we were supposed to become was horrifying, something none of us wanted. I was particularly afraid of it. The opportunity for rebellion and provocation outweighed any offering of payoff. Becoming simply successful would have been too simple and none of us wanted to go that route.

I'd connected to punk rock in the way that it had taken down and defeated its forefathers. Like an unruly teenager who comes up and defiantly shows their family what's up. As teenagers, that's our job. The misogyny and the clichés of hard rock had been challenged on my clock. I was on that side of history, and in that way I was repulsed by what old rock music represented. Groupies, backstage blow jobs, the hierarchy of the male ego, all of it suggested a dinosaur of an era that I'd never felt part of. The sheer memory or nostalgia of what rock had been minimized the focus and outcome of what we had worked on for so long to achieve. There was an individuality and an art to what we pushed, an agenda with a direction and a confusion that didn't involve history or clichés. With the guitar, though, things got complicated.

There is no denying the power of the chunka-chunka guitar. It is a sound of beef and power, a heralding of stance and presence that suggests might. A mountain of declaration. An anchor dropped and a victory flag waved.

Instantly relatable and undeniably familiar, it is a tool and a crux.

Mostly because of the guitar, the band was thrown into a category. Even the suggestion of categorical was offensive to me. I didn't want to be categorized. There were notions of that world that I appreciate for sure. Like Metallica, for instance. Metallica felt sincere. I'd embraced what they were, and the force and the audacity of their craft. Theirs was a power, a movement of derelicts that I could *kind of* relate to. But the baggage. I'd gone to a show of theirs back when I had dreadlocks, my hair tied in a bandanna on the top of my head, wearing a long john'd red button-up underwear set and a yellow, rubber rain jacket. For no effect, I was just dressed that way, and the Metallica fans shouted at me like I'd hurt them, like I was offending them or intentionally baiting them. They yelled *faggot* and let me know I wasn't welcome in their camp. So we had that. Not to blame the band or their intentions, but kids yelling *faggot* came from that place, from that forum. There was only so far I could go in the world of hard rock with that sort of a mindset on the table.

Attention is attention and I tend to like it despite everything, but all of the accolades from people I didn't respect shifted the trajectory of the band. We had legitimately started as an art project. I'd been reaching, we'd all been reaching higher than that, but still. The yield of what we started to get was some real low-hanging fruit. The fruit was bountiful, there was lots of it and it was overripe, it was just the easy stuff, more accessible. Soft with wormholes. The thing that made us different in that particular realm of rock was the keyboards, in the midst of all the pummel of thunder and power and macho, there was the haunt and the beauty of the keyboards. And that guy was gay. I didn't really clock it at the time, but I was the thing that made us not-them. I was the different spice in the mix that turned it into something else. While that's special, it's also troubling and it was a responsibility I reluctantly took on.

28

. . . .

After finishing a record that was complicated and challenging, we said yes to the Guns and the Roses with Metallica tour, opening up for that. It was an opportunity that everyone was behind and excited about. The sheer amount of people we'd be playing in front of was mind-boggling. The record we had finished was called *Angel Dust*. The dichotomy of the heavenly moniker for the ugliest of drugs made a statement in my head. The cover art would be a glorious white swan in Hallmark beauty taking off from the surface of a beautiful lake. Courtney tried to steal the title from me, but the idea of the title was mine. The record was a response to the universal reaction we'd received as a band, where we'd been, who we'd touched, and what was expected of us. Someone from our record company had come and listened to what we'd recorded as we were finishing the album and muttered, "Well, I hope none of you have bought houses." The thing was we all had.

The tour was the biggest circus on earth. The Guns and the Roses were under scrutiny for a song in which they'd used the N-word and the faggot word in the same sentence. The singer looked like a possum. He was so famous, they were all so famous. Everyone liked to imitate that ugly swivel dance he did. How I took it all in and related to it was complicated.

I'd pack up everything and enough drugs to last a couple of days and head out on a tour. There was something cathartic to throwing my body around, bruising myself real good. To cringe or flex or scrunch my body in an extreme was the only time I could feel. There was an exercise to feeling, the dope became accustomed to numbing my body and my body had to relearn how to feel, that was how the sickness ebbed and flowed. The grate of the flooring of those massive stages when we played was cold and metal in thick rows. I'd throw myself onto it and push my face into it and see through the grate.

Metallica was as perfect as a band could be to us. They showed us encouragement and support when it was unorthodox and didn't make sense to do that. A lot of it hinged on loyalty. Their bass player, Cliff, who died in an accident on tour, had grown up with Mike, the drummer, and Jim. I remember him really well. His was a crazy spirit, an odd wizard in that world, he moved his head in an insane way as he played. He had ridiculous long hair and bell bottoms, big, like huge swaths of denim around his ankles. He and Mike had seen the last performance of the Sex Pistols at Winterland. When he passed away the rest of his band took us on, in his memory it felt like.

Paradox that loyalty with the tone of the backstage village. There were so many boobs. Millions of boobs. There were themes for the parties after the shows. Hawaiian Luau. The Great Pyramids. The Great Gatsby (I made that one up). How it worked was there were two crews and identical production lines working simultaneously. While one was dealing with the show at hand in one city, the second crew was in the next city prepping. Part of the prep was the crew of the Guns and the Roses canvassing the strip clubs and malls for boobs. They'd pass out band laminates to the strippers and women they'd meet. By the time the band showed up, the backstage was filled with these women, a psychotically flashy bombardment of that local flavor.

We would get to the venues early, we always played first, we'd hide in a trailer and play our show and leave. Jim, our guitar player, would stick around and indulge in whatever things were happening because that's who he was. The rest of us would leave and I'd go out on the streets of the city and try to find dope. That meant going to a part of town that was unfamiliar and peppered with drug users. I was good at finding it. In the same way I could find men cruising, read their body habits and language, I could pick out the neighborhoods where the junkies were. It's human behavior. I'd look but mostly I'd just get sick and wait and go back to a hotel room and bide the slow time.

The hotel room is a perfect holding cell. No one knows. Sprawled out naked on a crumpled bed and watching the digital clock. A tray from room service on the floor with overturned bowls, a spilled glass with melted ice and an old lemon wedge, a burnt spoon and a syringe, no one can get in. From here, from inside a locked room, time lasts forever.

The wait time became less and less as shows were canceled, and it's hard to explain. There was a huge amount of drama for a bunch of straight boys. The singer of the Guns and the Roses would have the stage blessed before shows, in the afternoon of the night of performances. A psychic woman would show up early, one close to him who he trusted, she was in robes and she'd feel it out for him and get a sense of spirit and what was to come for the night. It was her job to purify the stage. I saw her a couple times. She'd stalk the stage with something burning and clean out the bad spirits. I'd watch her from a distance. I guess she missed things sometimes. People got injured onstage during the shows by pyrotechnics mishaps, other times there were riots. Sometimes she'd just get a bad feeling and the show would be canceled. In situations like that, we'd pack up and go home for days and I'd get high again. For three or four days before going out and reconvening and starting the cycle again. It couldn't be written in a more punishing fashion.

I'd still be sick and Jim would be at the baggage terminal in his Mustang with enough dope on some foil to make me better on the ride home. I could feel my stomach changing as I did it. The bubbling stopped and the settling started and I'd lean my head against the window and look outside and almost throw up in gratitude, watching gray San Francisco. I'd get back to my house on the top of the Castro with the beautiful view and lie on the sofa and get high. The girl on the motorcycle had already been there, I'd get loaded and turn off everything. I'd kept the needles from Jim, we would just smoke the drug together, but I'd find them in the city and had learned how to cook the drug and soak it up through the cotton from a cigarette filter and inject it into my own arm.

I'd had it done for me before I taught myself to do it on my own. Using the white heroin from New York, hoarded paper bindles I'd stock up before leaving town, that didn't need cooking. I'd mix it with water in a spoon or else a bottle cap and suck it up through the eye of the needle. The concoction was clear so that when the blood from my arm was pulled back into it, I could see it in the syringe. The tar from California was a dark brown and the blood was hard to see. The romance and witchery of it was chilling.

The tour went on like that. Canceled shows and trips home and dopesick and high. As far as I knew I was getting away with things and the band wasn't really paying attention. I told myself I was doing what I needed to do. The thing about touring is the only time that's absolutely pertinent is that forty-five minutes onstage. All of the rest of it is just biding time. That forty-five minutes I did my job, but the band as a whole wasn't making a lot of affect. We would watch the numbers of our record being sold and there really wasn't much of a correlation between playing those huge shows and selling records. We were another ring in that circus, the opening act of jesters or clowns who weren't taken seriously. No one really liked us and that took its toll.

We resented the lack of attention and the environment and who it was coaxing us to become and we started acting out. We talked shit in the press and made things up and disrespected people who helped us. I'd lift up the boom stand as we played, the crooked thing that held up my microphone at my keyboard, and swing it, smash it onto the grating of the floor of the stage in a heroic swing of an arc. For no reason other than it made me feel. We all started to behave that way and got in trouble for it.

29

....

Provocation and stirring up shit always came easy. It was how I grew up and my intuition for it was second nature. We got to a show in the outskirts of some weird city on the Guns and the Roses tour and our manager from Los Angeles was there. He'd flown in at the request of the band to have a meeting. With us and the band. We all walked into a trailer that was housing the singer and the guitar player named Slash and we knew it was coming. It made sense they'd be pissed. We were literally making things up to people in the press to create a reaction and we were making fun of their institution, what they did, who they were, the music they made. All this after having been embraced by them and taken under their wing, so to speak, and offered the opportunity to open up for that circus. We shit on the opportunity, we'd been at that game for as long as they had but we had such a different perspective. We were smart and sarcastic and disrespectful. In all the best ways. I can't shake the pride I still feel from the distance we tried to create between them and us.

We had to wait till after the show was over to talk. We'd always leave immediately after we'd played so this was different. We stayed and watched their whole show and it felt like homework.

"It's not cool, man," was basically what was said. The singer said it and we all looked at our feet and agreed. Billy was taking the blame and the rest of us just nodded. There wasn't a leg to stand on. Our manager held his chin and kept standing up and sitting back down. It wasn't clear whether or not we'd be asked to leave the tour. What we offered the circus in terms of credibility seemed almost worth keeping us around, but then honestly not. They didn't need us. For whatever reason, the singer asked us to stay on and we apologized. There was a collective exhale and we stood up and a man from the production in floppy sweat shorts, a fanny pack, a lot of laminates, and a walkie-talkie came in and whispered something into the singer's ear. He looked at the rest of us through the side of his narrow piggy eyes and said, "Y'all wanna check something out?"

We followed him to another trailer, part of the mix and the compound, there were so many trailers housing a hundred different tasks. The door of the trailer opened and we filed up the two steps that were the same metal as the grating of the stage floor and into a bright room, fluorescent and harsh and silent. There was a bed, a sort of a hospital bed, simple and collapsible and not sturdy, and one woman was on top of another, licking her pussy that was shaved and tan. They had long polished nails, both of them, and a scrunchy had fallen from one of their heads to the floor. The only sound in the trailer was the whir of a camera that another person from one of the other bands was videotaping the women with. Her tongue moved fast and sternly, the way you'd never want to be kissed.

We started to scream, incredulous, and Mike P hit the wall of the trailer, spanking it loudly with his open palm, shouting. We were saying, "No way, no way," in a lot of different ways. The girls stopped almost imperceptibly and one looked at us impatiently like a bored cashier at a convenience store and took us in from head to toe, not smiling. We were pushed out of the trailer by the man with the laminates.

It was scenarios like these. A million different variations of that same ugly scene. A twisted realm of misogyny and entitlement that reeked of cat food. Something around that time became too much. It was the energy of the men and the numbness of the situations they'd encourage. The women were treated like dolls. The environments were abused and I was alone in myself with my gay and my drugs and the complacency with what I was doing, what we were doing as a band. There were so many stupid looks on so many fucking stupid faces and really bad fashion and dumb banter and ugly-man energy and poor design decisions when the money was clearly there to make beautiful ones. Women were taken advantage of, the hierarchy of privileged men was distinct and applauded. An older stance of greed and need and abuse was being held up as a revival, a nostalgic nod back to a time that had never worked in the first place. It was a lot of older men pulling the strings, but the young men were following in their footsteps and it trickled out into the world, what they were doing. I didn't want any part of it.

Who can sit well with that horror?

30
....

Lance Loud was an icon in my periphery. He was the son in the original reality television series called *An American Family*. The show chronicled the growth of a California family over the course of some years in the early 1970s. In the trajectory of palm trees and family values and meals around the table was the coming out of Lance as a gay teen. The producers hadn't known, hadn't seen it coming, and the whole show pivoted on his journey. He acted out in the public eye when the media hated him. He was loved by our people and he later moved to New York and started a band with my sister's friend Kristian called the Mumps. He became friends with Andy Warhol and eventually moved back to LA and wrote for magazines like the *Advocate* and *Out* and the other one I can't remember its name. Gay magazines.

Over the course of that big-big-big tour I'd been on in America and in the face of all that ugliness, Lance asked to interview me for the *Advocate*. I honestly didn't think twice, I said yes immediately. I'd never spoken of my sexuality in that way, in the press. The immersion and being in the realm of that camp of misogyny and dude vibes pointed me in an obvious and reactionary direction. I'd been assimilating as many aspects of gay culture as I could without being part of it. Which feels weird to type.

Onstage and in photos I had basically portrayed every character of the Village People, shy of the Native American, and in my head it was a defiance to the norm and a nod to what I'd aspire to without consciously saying that to myself. Those references were important to me in easing myself out of the closet. I was a cowboy, I was a cop, I was the leather guy in mirrored shades, I was anyone but my gay self.

I've learned over time to not have to apologize for this process. It is and remains the lone and solitary decision and direction of the gay individual after years and episodes of so much doubt and delusion and vulnerability and misrepresentation and exclusionary practicing. I was the sum of my parts of received and absorbed discrimination. The dichotomy was that I lived in San Francisco, in the mix of an accepting and open-minded village that only championed the left of center and the marginalized. In my head, though, that route was too easy. Which is kind of a cop-out but it felt absolutely too predictable, the notion of the piano-playing boy of a family of sisters who moved to San Francisco to be gay. I won't apologize but it feels bad. Billy especially had been my best friend and work partner and comrade in crime since we were little and I'd really shut him out. Not being open and honest with him set a precedent in our adult relationship that never went back and I'm sorry to not have had the opportunity that my honesty would have inspired. We'd have a different friendship if I'd known how to be honest about who I was.

I'd never had a gay hero to look up to. There was no one in my young world who made it easy. I'd loved Elton John when I was little. He played piano, there was a kinship I intuited. I heard him on the radio, I turned it up and pushed my head against the speaker, hoping. He talked about being married and dispelled any rumors of his being gay. And he had an English accent. Even Freddie Mercury wasn't gay at the time. There was a quote that Queen had used about doing the math: four long-haired men in tight pants singing opera music in a band called Queen. But they didn't come out and say it. It was a time when we were expected to read between the lines. Even if it was obvious, it certainly wasn't declared proudly. Village People said they didn't want to say either way because they didn't want to lose any fans they might have had who didn't approve. It was only shame, so much of it, so prevalent, gay was a bad thing and something to hide. Even later, much later, Michael Stipe, Bob Mould. There were rumors but no one came out proudly and said it. The secrecy and the downplaying made it all the more shameful.

I was in a dark place. I had gone back and forth so many times on that tour from using drugs to getting sick to high to withdrawals. There was a window and a light coming through a crack that offered a splinter of relief in the context of mental health and it was coming out and letting that splash in the face of the hetero world of rock that I was immersed in. Saying yes to Lance Loud in a proclamation of a gay agenda wasn't encouraged, it was discouraged. One of my managers, the Christian one, tried to talk me out of it.

I did the interview with Lance on the phone and we took pictures in my bedroom on the hill in San Francisco. I wore white briefs and bondage wrist straps of leather and my eyebrow had been pierced, my hair was fucked up, I was high on dope, standing on the mattress of my bed upstairs in socks. It was on a break from tour and I posed in a way I hadn't. A posture. A connection to where the image was headed.

There were moments like these that I remember photographically. I can see the photo of me with Nanny on the front lawn of the old house; she'd picked an orange from a tree we knew not to eat from. Her face was screwed up into a pucker from the sour of the fruit and I was crying in a two-piece, short, royal-blue suit. I remember that or I remember the photograph, holding it and looking at myself, I'm not sure which. So many instances in life are just remembering the visit of the memory. The photographs of me that day getting my picture taken, showing my version of gay, are triumphant and sad, I can see that my eyes are fucked up. Maybe most people wouldn't see that.

That bedroom in that home in that neighborhood in that city at that time and all of the eyes I'd come to know. Some eyes are stories and some eyes are dead. Some eyes are short lists for things done. The eyes chronicle it all. Jim's eyes were scrunched up in a tired and drugged-out way, watered down and washed of color. Sober eyes were twinkly and singing, captivated and sparkling. Eyes on acid are alive and overwhelmed, the pupil huge, the black almost overtaking the iris. Heroin eyes are pinned and dead. The pupil goes away to a tiny speck. The blue of my dad's eyes as he got sick grew lighter and grayer, softer than blue and then not soft at all. The chemo took the color out of them. What a gift it is to look a person in the eye.

Lance Loud sold the article and interview he did with me not only to the *Advocate* but to a bunch of European rock magazines. That wasn't part of the deal, Lance. It wasn't what we had discussed and it pissed me off, but he's since passed and it's not really important. It was him making some money off the world that we'd talked about taking down, but okay, Lance. The world needed to hear a queer agenda anyway and the story of me being gay and coming out reached ears it wouldn't have.

There was a legion of fans in the world who loved the opportunity to support me. There was a pride and a willingness among the kids that was sweet and surprising. The catapult of faith and conviction and honesty resounded. I'd spoken my truth and it was heard as that. Kids we'd see every day were in it for exactly that reason, the diversity, the challenge, the unconventionality of a bunch of misfits. I love them for that.

The true payoff and beauty of the moment was the gay kids. Queer kids who cried, they'd approach me shyly and tell their stories. Being true and honest with yourself and your friends and your family wasn't easy for most of those kids. To love that music and take part in that world was a challenge as queers. That era had homophobia bred right into itself; the threads of that scene, that culture were based on a patriarchy and a heterosexual plethora that hadn't shifted in a long time. Fag jokes and insinuations that pushed our people down or to the side, these were the suggestions we lived in, all of us. Butting our heads against it, I know, I know. Queer kids would cry and I'd hug them. It didn't get better than that.

The band and I never talked about me coming out. If we did, I don't remember the conversations. This doesn't sit well with me, the neglect of talking about it. In the absence of real we stir the neglect. Behind the curtains it's easy to ignore the stage. The best of puppet masters work well with the strings without looking at the marionette. That's a ridiculous analogy but we were all busy. I was busy and I should have made that conversation a reality. The attempt on my part of making it look like it was a casual decision, that's maybe the core of the sickness. Because it wasn't casual. It was huge. I didn't acknowledge it as huge and that sent an erred message to the core of my life at that point, my band.

31

....

I had bought a house. The house was on a street called Eagle, down from a park called Kite Hill. I lived there alone but with Jim, who still had the apartment on the edge of the Tenderloin. I'd drive my motorcycle to the YMCA downtown in the mornings and work out and smoke heroin on tinfoil as the day turned. The back and forth between the drug and not-the-drug loped along like a limp.

San Francisco was still mostly magical, sooty and desirable, cheap and disgusting. The Pixies came to San Francisco and I drove Kim Deal on the back of my motorcycle with no helmet on, it was before the helmet law, to a liquor store in the Tenderloin. She'd been hungry and bought a small can of Vienna sausages. She was staying in a hotel on the edge of a dirty neighborhood where Kurt and Courtney stayed soon after. Nirvana happened big quickly but it was still in the upward trajectory before people really knew. The hotel was kind of a haven for bands. There was birdsong piped from the outdoor speakers around a lima-bean swimming pool. Kurt was wearing a slip of Courtney's and had all of his laminates, like six of them, around his neck as he roamed the outside hallways of the hotel looking for ice. He was being laughed at by a couple rocker kids who didn't know better.

I need to look up years. I have no idea what hap-

pened when, I've never known the year it was and honestly sometimes stop for too long when I need to write
down the year it is. That Nirvana show at the Warfield
was magic. It was 1991, I looked this up. The sound and
their set was pure chaos. Impossible things were happening onstage. Things collided and banged and were broken,
the sound of it glorious. After the show, in the downstairs
of the backstage were nooks and seats and everyone from
the audience was buzzing around and Kurt was sitting
there, by himself at a small table, splayed out on a stupid
chair all alone. I sat down and we talked about anything
but the show. I knew better than to speak of that.

On heroin you think you're getting away with everything. As much as my scheming and paranoid mind didn't
want to admit it, everyone knew but nothing was ever
said. Other than my family. My mother chose to ignore
the addiction. Can you even imagine the joy and the own-
ership of a mother who taught her son to play piano when
the reward of an actual career nudges its way into his life?
And in public? On the cover of magazines? Her religious
friend had sent me a letter after reading an interview in
which one of us had referenced jerking off in a weird way,
and she wrote that my mother was embarrassed by my
words. It wasn't true, Michelle. My mom had a real high
tolerance for that kind of stuff.

Even though the pride was prevalent and abundant,
the heroin was too much for anyone to take on. Jim and
I were doing it too much and we'd throw the world away
in a second by making the decision to score. Everything
was okay. It was and then it wasn't, and what we were
doing behind closed doors became a thing. Friends started
to fall off and intervene.

If someone doesn't call you out on your shit when you're acting out, are you even doing anything wrong? Getting sick was the ultimate punishment and was the only reason to stop, the avoidance of that. In the mix of being sick and wanting more, there was only the drive to feel better and that would outweigh anything else. Social responsibility and promises and what I knew I should be doing became nonissues. There were only reasons to get high and then no reasons to not get high.

Heroin makes you forget things, it's part of the process, it's actually the point, it's why we do the drug in the first place and what makes it special. Trying to remember now feels counterintuitive, I worked so hard to make sure I didn't remember things and here I sit, doing my best to bring the details back.

I was standing at an open refrigerator, I'd done speed to try to fix myself in the throes of the withdrawals from heroin, and I fell, grabbing on to the inside of the refrigerator door. The condiments all dropped to the floor and broke, the sound was loud, the cold metal piece of refrigerator I held in my hand as I tried to get up off the floor. Jim and Alisa came running and I couldn't explain anything. I stayed on the kitchen floor as if I'd gone there on purpose and they eventually let me be and walked away, the light from the refrigerator illuminating me splayed out on the dirty linoleum floor. We'd gone without dope for almost two days and I was getting really sick, but we went to a show anyway in Jim's Mustang. On the way to the club we saw the dope girl on the motorcycle underneath a wet freeway overpass and I tried to pull her over.

What was it about the burden of the sickness that made us feel grown up? We were older and struggled with issues like withdrawal. That back and forth, being high and then sick, it wasn't a place for children. We were going to lengths. We lived hard. We pushed ourselves to feel things. There was pride in it then, a badge of honor, a stepping-up of person. It feels like macho bullshit as I write it and it really make no sense, but I kind of understand where proud men go when they boast.

In Europe there are ways to find drugs. Italy is a snap, I can't explain my nose for it. I'd find it easily. Mostly train stations but sometimes just town squares. I was good at navigating the score, I was only ripped off once in Amsterdam. The packet I bought wasn't dirt but it was something like dirt. It definitely wasn't heroin though I kept snorting it until it was all gone, hoping. The memories of getting my drugs back to the hotel room are comforting and fond. Buying chemicals on the streets from filthy brethren with dirty nails and ingesting the drugs, trusting with an open heart. So many times over I should have been dead.

In Los Angeles the heroin was brown and tar and smelled like burnt sugar. It was sticky and dark, sometimes hard like an amethyst, other times softer to the touch like chewed gum. It depended on the batch. It came in balloons, baby, primary-colored balloons tied off or inside out onto themselves. My sisters had found the different-colored, spent balloons in the filter vent of the dryer in the downstairs laundry room of our family house. It's how they knew I was using again. There was no arguing or talking my way out of that.

In New York the heroin was white powder and sold in Alphabet City in folded wax-paper envelopes, rectangles small enough to fit into the palm of your hand. The envelopes were stamped with stencils, the different breeds of dope named accordingly. Freeball. Supercycle. Listerine. Power Ranger. Ninja. Different dealers would chant the names of different strains as we shopped for it. "Crystal Drano, Crystal Drano." Then another man, "Daffy Duck, looking for Daffy Duck?" The man would press the envelopes into our hands and push us off, like two magnets facing the wrong way, barely touching, then quickly apart.

The first time I heard about heroin I was young, maybe nine or ten. My sisters and I had taken an interest in the *Los Angeles Times*, we were encouraged by our parents. A new family rule was that we had to bring to the dinner table a topic of conversation from an article we'd read in the newspaper that day. An article. I love my parents for this. I read about Patty Hearst and shared her drama with my family for weeks. She was kidnapped, she was missing, her parents, her roommates in the dorm, Steve her fiancé, the SLA, the Hibernia Bank, it took up most of a season. When she changed her name to Tania I cried. I was rooting for the underground and her role in it was important to me.

In that mix of research when I was reading the paper, I'd seen an article about heroin and the Lower East Side of Manhattan. There was a photograph of dope being lowered in a bucket on a rope from the third floor of a tenement building down to a line of customers on the sidewalk. There were twelve or twenty people in line, they'd take turns putting their money in the bucket, it would be raised to a window above and come back down with the heroin. The mechanics of it fascinated me, it was very *Swiss Family Robinson*, the tree house with its levers and troughs and pullies. I couldn't wait to get to New York, even at that age. The article in the paper pointed out the diversity of the buyers and the photograph showed that: a businessman, someone in hospital scrubs, a tracksuit, a gray man in a wheelchair. I imagined myself in the mix.

I looked for it in New York but I never saw the bucket. We'd buy our dope from a man in Alphabet City. Courtney had schooled me on scoring in downtown LA. We'd driven down to Skid Row in my mother's car and had pulled over into a parking lot that was closed, the chain around the lot was down on the ground and we drove over it. There was a cluster of men. Courtney's passenger window was down and she negotiated a deal. The price was fifty dollars and then after the exchange it had changed to sixty dollars and Courtney wasn't having it.

"Drive, Ros, drive," she hissed. The balloons of drugs were clutched in her hand in her lap and I started to reverse the car, slowly navigating out of the deal. The Mexican man's hand still engaged through the passenger window.

"Stop, Ros, stop." I looked over and he had grabbed a thick handful of her hair, his fingers entwined tightly down to her roots, to her scalp, holding on tight. Her head was cocked, her neck taut, she was wincing and holding up a twenty. How to explain why this is so much funnier than it was threatening. He took it and let go of her hair and spat at the car. We drove off and got high.

Maynard and Dan lived in New York near Max Fish. We'd buy our dope and rigs and go up to their apartment. They gave me a key, just a key, no chain, no ribbon, a naked key in my pocket. It felt casual and New York, a sense of pride to carry that key. By the time I was using needles, finding a syringe in the Lower East Side was as easy as scoring dope. It was usually like a one-stop shop but sometimes you'd have to go to a second vendor to buy the needle.

It was hot, a New York summer, and we were in the apartment, sitting on the edge of an open tub where we'd hose the back of our necks down with the shower nozzle after a speedball. The feeling was amazing. A rush that snaps your head alert and makes your arms tingle into a sweet exhale of exhilaration that doubles you over. Dan's Japanese wife sat and watched. She said small things as she watched us, quietly to Dan; none of us understood the Japanese. I don't remember her name. Kyoko.

We'd gone back to the apartment after I'd played a big show at the Ritz in New York City and they'd come backstage. I saw Dan putting food from the deli tray in his pocket and pretended that I hadn't. A stack of sliced cheese, he wrapped it in a napkin. Later on that night, I don't remember much more than being slapped hard in the face and I was all wet. My shoes still on, my pants soaked through, my T-shirt ripped down from the neck-line and my legs bent weirdly beneath me in the tub. There was the flash of the light of an ambulance through the window outside, the rest of us were down on the floor with the lights off, hiding. I'd OD'd and they'd called 911 before I came to as they slapped me and put the shower hose on me. They'd been able to revive me and they didn't want the paramedics or police involved. We didn't need them after all, so we stayed on the ground like that until the ambulance lights stopped flashing. I don't remember a lot more. I had died. No one likes to talk about their mistakes.

The next night my band played a second show at the

same venue and I'd wanted to score again, but the friends discouraged it. I remember quipping, "Yeah, I died last night and came back to life," with no humor or sarcasm. It just was that and I wasn't being dramatic or funny. That might have been my last chapter of shooting dope in New York City. There was a music video we made in Queens at some point where I hid in a shower stall in a dressing room trying to find a vein. Maybe that was the last time. The timeline gets fuzzy when you're doing your best to forget.

The good feeling of the drug stops being as consistent. It takes more dope to get there and it just doesn't economize. There's never enough. There's too little or never enough, never too much. The equation of quitting and the science of how long it takes to get through the withdrawals gets tricky as you get into it. It started as little more than losing a night's sleep after running out. My body would twitch in an uncomfortable way and my legs would spasm at night. The sleep wasn't easy but I was young and I'd get over it. Progressively it became a lot worse. I wouldn't sleep for three days, stomachaches, uncontrollable kicking legs in bed. Everything smelled bad and tasted worse. Cigarettes were no solace. The key word I think is restless, no rest, less rest than usual, a million different things that word implies. Thoughts don't stick, the body kicks, the muscles are taut but can't stretch enough. Every time I'd stop, these feelings would get worse. It only made sense to keep doing it.

In Guam after Hawaii I'd left the stage before the encore and told the band to do the last songs without me. I blamed fish, sushi, but everyone knew. There were four days off in a hotel room in Guam before going to Japan. It seemed like it took four days to get close to normal on the other side of the habit. The first day you slept, the second day was the start, the third, the horror, the fourth, the beginning of the end. Someone in rehab later told me Guam was the heroin capital of the world. Army vets ended up there with bad habits. I hadn't known. It was an army base to me, we were on a sort of resort ground. Day two into withdrawals I rented a tennis racket from the front desk and tried to hit a ball against a wall, in shorts, sweating and convulsing. I saw someone from the band watching me from a window. It had never been worse.

At night some of the band and our crew were going to a cockfight and I made myself join them. I was on day three, my body hurt and I couldn't stop sweating. We took a hotel van and got dropped off. I was sick and couldn't sit still, my legs were cramping and I was nauseous. It looked like a tent revival I'd seen on television, an immense orange canvas covering, the entrance and perimeters of which were flapping in a warm, tropical wind. Light came from out of it, it glowed like a movie set. Evangelists or professional wrestlers or circus people, I'd almost forgotten why we'd gone and what to expect. There were insanely pungent smells everywhere. Overly seasoned popcorn, sawdust, shit, mold, too much cologne. I separated myself from the band up in the aluminum stands. Chickens in the center ring were being thrown at each other and encouraged to fight. The chickens were mean and angry, like straight men, puffing out their chicken chests, showing off. Bets were being made and men were shouting, waving wads of cash at each other. Fat people drank beer in the stands and I wandered up to the top, behind everyone, up high in the back row. Down below, behind the stands, on a table, a man smoking a cigarette with dirty hands was sewing up a chicken's neck, cut open from a fight. Another man pinned the chicken's wings down as it tried to flap away. They were getting it ready for a new fight. I'd never been sicker.

32

. . . .

It could have ended there. It should have ended there. It didn't end there. Things got so much worse. If only it was someone else's story and not mine. I'm not sure if the telling would be the same. My father got a stomachache. He was coming to meet me on tour in Prague and then he was going to travel on the bus with me to England where the band would play a festival. Reading Festival. It was a proud moment for me and it was really cool he'd be involved. I talked to him on a phone in a production office at a venue and watched the scenario playing out. He couldn't come, he told me, his stomach was bothering him. Like in a movie, the dry cough that happens on-screen and always, inevitably becomes something bigger. It's so obvious it's insulting. By the time I flew back to Los Angeles after the festival, everyone knew but me. My sisters were at the airport when I landed and were all crying outside of baggage claim near the white zone that was for the loading and unloading of passengers only. It was unstoppable, there was no preventing it and it would happen fast. He had pretty much two or three months.

I'd wanted to take the reins and steer us. It would have fit the story so nicely to be able to have stepped in and assumed that role, the one of the only son taking on the legacy of the dying patriarch. Like the replacement of the king in a royal family. In actuality it didn't need to be me. In turn, I wasn't capable of taking it on. I went right back to dope. Immediately. I couldn't get it fast enough. I got in the family car, drove to the dope dealer, and sat in the car, parked illegally in front of a fire hydrant in the sleepy blocks below Hollywood. I fixed myself, tied off my arm, shot up, and breathed deep. I leaned the driver's seat back with the lever and closed my eyes and didn't cry. My aim was just to get through it.

I took my dad to Montana because he had some sort of notion of being a cowboy. He'd been on trips with friends, travel trips, campout trips, and we had lots of pictures of him on a horse. Pictures my mother framed later and hung in her downstairs room that used to be Catherine's bedroom. They'd ride and do overnights and a chef rode with them and made chili and stuff. He had a cowboy hat and an elaborate belt buckle, too pretty for cowboys. It was silver and gold, Black Hills gold, *Buckaroos* written in a calligraphy. That's what they'd called their group. He had friends in Montana he hadn't seen for a long time, so me and my mom and my dad flew there. I wasn't working, the tour had ended and I was basically available in a way that my sisters weren't. They all had jobs. I didn't bring enough dope and had more sent to me in the motel we stayed at in Bozeman. The FedEx guy was in the parking lot and talking to a worker from the motel, they knew each other and he was taking his time dropping off the package as I watched from behind a curtain in my room, sweating and shaking.

We visited my dad's old friend and his wife, who made dinner for us, and I played their piano dramatically, like I was scoring the chapter. We drove to Old Faithful and I went to the bathroom stall and pulled water into the syringe from the toilet to shoot up with. I took footage with my video camera of my dad riding a horse in a pen and got real dramatic with my voice-over.

"There's my dad," I was saying.

I wish I had that footage still. As overwrought and drug-fueled as it was, the footage was real, it had happened.

My sisters knew the score pretty much right from the get-go. They'd found the spoons and the foil under the dresser in my bedroom and then the spent colored balloons in the vent of the family dryer. They intervened and told me to go back to San Francisco. My drug use was complicating the complications and trauma of my father's passing and I was no good to anyone. I lied and pretended I was getting help. I made up a therapist name, Tom, and told them we were working on things weekly on the phone. I said I was going to meetings and I'd leave in the family car and sit somewhere and nod off.

I held my father's hand at Cedar Sinai as he got worse. He wanted to be home. He'd done the chemo and the radiation and he was tired of it all. I remember the chemo doctor, a woman, hugging my sisters but not me. Maybe I hadn't made the initial gesture to move in for a hug, I'm not sure. There was talk and hope of coffee enemas, Indonesian treatments that could possibly help, but then an older doctor's sad eyes that just told us what he knew we knew. *Just let it happen* seems like a cop-out but there is solace, finally. Just let it happen. We did that. We checked him out of the hospital and rented a bed from people who delivered it, set it up in the den, and moved the sofa to the garage. We left the photo albums that had been under the sofa on the carpet where they'd been, they were now under the hospital bed my father was scheduled to die in.

The band had done a song for a compilation record with a crew of Samoan rappers from Carson and we'd agreed to make a video with them for the project. I knew my band was on to me and I'd surrounded myself on the day of the video shoot with an armor of children, Sammy and Leilani, my two favorite kids from down the street that I'd grown up on. They were eight and thirteen. I loved them and I'd brought them to the shoot, making it difficult for the band to get me alone. There was an outhouse where I shot up. A porta potty. The manager of the band was there on the set in a trailer we were using as a dressing room and eventually I was corralled into it and we all sat down to have the talk.

It's honestly a nice talk to have when it happens. It was a disgusting and inevitable resolve. To be able to go with honesty after lying for so long is a relief, to just let it flow. To give in and cut the bullshit and take a break from the lies. The front of it is threatening and scary and real, but then it just unfolds. By itself, naturally. Everyone involved is on board with the repair, the fix, the goodwill of it all, and for a second I felt like a star and appreciated the attention, as wayward as it was. People believed in me and I believed in myself. I wanted to take an actual bow. I was out-of-my-mind fucked up.

It was early in the morning when I got home to my family's house. We'd been shooting the video all night and I'd been on the phone with Courtney throughout it all. She and Kurt were at a similar place in their habits, we all understood each other. She'd made reservations for the three of us to check into a rehab facility in Long Beach. They'd had three beds and could facilitate. We were all going to get well together. It seemed feasible. I'd reached the point where the withdrawals were going to be too intense to do it on my own. My sister Catherine had just got to town and she was in the kitchen, carrying her first daughter, Michaela, who was not a year old. I hadn't seen her for a while.

"Is she ours?" I asked. I don't know why I said that.

It was a crazy dichotomy, Dad dying in the den and that funny, fat toddler smiling, me in the middle, dopesick and stuck.

My dad was sympathetic and understanding and noble and patient with me. So many things. He always liked Courtney. He got her, he recognized her genius and thought she was hilarious. The notion of Kurt and Courtney and me in rehab was an adventure to him. My sisters were stern and my mom had other things to worry about. Her husband was dying.

Once I laid out the plan to my family and established how it was to go down, the phone rang. It was Courtney, all pragmatic, matter-of-fact. Change of plans. She said that on the phone to me, "Change of plans, Ros." She'd bought enough Valium for the three of us to last a week and get through withdrawals. They'd bought three tickets to Seattle. We'd fly up there and coast through being sick on Valium.

"I just told my family that we're going to rehab," I said.

We sat in silence for a while. It was a moment. A long silence as I held the phone and closed my eyes.

"Maybe you should," she said.

My sister Stephanie drove me alone to the rehab in Long Beach. I remember my forehead on the glass of the window in the passenger seat. Stephanie had taken the day off work. I told her I felt like a loser and she listed all the friends we had who had gotten clean. I kept thinking about Jeff McDonald, the older brother in Redd Kross. He and Charlotte were sober and I'd gone to their wedding at their home trying to not use. I'd painted my nails elaborately. Their home was in the hills and Spanish, an example somehow of something that could be.

My head was empty and defeated, I felt nothing but a slow burn of time ticking, I was still high from my last shot. The drugs had stopped working. The numbness was going to start to wear off, I wasn't anxious yet about the sick that was coming. I knew I had to lie about how much dope I'd been taking when I was admitted because they'd give me more meds if I said I'd been doing more drugs than I had. The come-down would be easier with more meds. I knew that and that's all I really knew.

33
·········

I fell down in a hospital hallway because I'd exaggerated too much when I'd told the nurses how much dope I'd been shooting. The meds they'd given me were way too strong, exactly what I'd asked for. I banged my face when I fell and they wanted to bandage it but I wouldn't let them. I was surly, I still am. There was dried blood on my face and the side of my head turned black and blue. My father made me clean the blood off myself when he came to visit me. He was right, I didn't need to make that point. He helped me scrub the blood off my face with a washcloth from the bathroom next to the hospital bed I slept in. I pushed back as he helped and tried to just throw the washcloth away, but he insisted on making it clean and hanging it back on the rack on the side of the sink to dry.

Three days into my withdrawals I stopped taking their meds. They were meant to go on for eight days but I was done. I could tell that earned me some credibility among the staff, I'd hoped for that, I wanted to be liked.

After a little more than a week in the facility I was over my withdrawals. I could see a little more clearly. I still couldn't sleep, I hadn't slept for over a week and didn't sleep honestly for a month. Kurt told me on the pay phone in the hall of the rehab that the point where I was was the point where he always left. Right after the withdrawals. I was contemplating leaving the agreed-upon month early, at like two weeks. I was feeling relatively pink and repaired.

"Maybe it's better to make it harder," he suggested.

I was in a really impressionable state and ended up taking his advice. I stayed in the rehab and two months later he was dead.

Out of the closet and clean. What could be more dull? The horror story is so much more intriguing before the resolve. I'm not a fan of closure. I prefer not being certain of things, not knowing what the problem is, being in the dark. Once the villain is revealed, the narrative loses its appeal for me and gets boring. Tedious and predictable, the motions of the story become simply a checklist to the finish line. There's too much credit and weight put in answers. I don't want anything tied up or resolved. I don't want to know answers. It's why tarot cards make me sick, there's too much reveal. What the fuck is wrong with *not* knowing? A smart man once recommended I leave the movie theater before things head in that direction. "Leave before the resolution," he told me. Things don't always get fixed, situations don't resolve, ends don't meet, the untying can sit for days, forever. Dirty stains don't always come off. Wounds don't heal. Bones don't always mend. Health doesn't improve and people die. Every single day.

In Santa Cruz in a dorm room at College Five, a hippie girl had read my tarot cards when I was younger. She was self-assured, it was a halftime break in her game of Dungeons & Dragons and she'd agreed to read my cards. I didn't respect the situation and Santa Cruz rubbed me the same wrong way that Berkeley did at the time. Too many wayward and optimistic hippies arguing among themselves, wanting to be heard. She asked me to choose a card as she flipped through her deck and I picked one that tried to slip into the folds of the others in her hand unnoticed. She turned that card over and revealed abundance, success. I wouldn't have to worry about anything, she assured me. I took that and haven't had my cards read since.

In the heights of the Tenderloin, walking to Deanne's car, we stopped to talk to a street psychic. We had aimed to drive to Marin and spend the day there. What we expected to find in Marin, I have no idea. An older woman was on the sidewalk with a turban and a deck of tarot cards laid out on an upside-down milk crate. Specific, wise, and content to engage, she said to me, "You . . . will always be lucky," and to Deanne, "You . . . will always have friends," and to Courtney, "You . . . will always be famous," and to Lisa Lusk, who was quiet and sad mostly, our goth friend who won tickets to rock shows too often on the radio, "You . . ." pausing dramatically, "will always be lonely."

It wasn't funny, it was a morose land mine of a road sign. It seems like we would have laughed more. We did later but it wasn't funny, it was dark. We took acid and got lost in the hills of Marin. We went to a winery, made fun of the world, and drove back to the city.

My father died. Cliff died. Kurt died. All at once. There's a rule of threes that people speak of. Fuck off.

On the patio in the sun of the rehab I'd checked into, Cliff was sitting on an indoor chair, one with fabric for a seat, the kind that surrounds a conference table. It wasn't meant for outdoors, that chair, and Cliff was sitting in it on a patio in the sun, oblivious. He was wearing long sleeves, we both were. No one could see our track marks with the long sleeves, we were both hiding them. I'd known him from shows and my crowd; he was gay but I had no idea he was a junkie. He had glasses, he looked a lot like Waldo without the stripes, and his body was that of a stork. His legs were tucked under themselves and crossed in a casual manner, his torso stretched high. His hands gesticulated animatedly, even in the throes of withdrawals. He'd been there for almost a week, I was a little bit behind him. Still, the kismet of the situation, we clutched each other, two gay men, hospitalized, sick for the overuse of drugs.

We got through the month of rehab together and became close in only a way two men in a hospital can. Like summer camp. We were both dying and the stakes were incredibly high. He'd tried lots of times to get clean. We shared a room in the rehab facility and dozed off side by side in our separate beds but never actually slept. I'd lie on my back, quietly, and hear him breathe deep and twist and roll around. I'd jerk off for a second or third time, then stretch my legs to impossible lengths as I came in an effort to make my body feel tired. We'd wake up and lie in bed and whisper and worry and speculate and conspire.

Secrets shared from bed to bed had never been more honest. I'd never been to summer camp before but in my head I'd imagine two best friends getting off the bus, arriving home. Arm in arm, backpacks on shoulders, sunburnt and dirty, having been through a shared time, a long shared time. We told each other things. He had a spot in the crook of his arm that never healed, it was like an open wound that he'd shoot dope into.

"I don't have to search for a vein. It just stays open and I shoot into it every time, it never fails."

This speak wasn't good. There was a danger in glamorizing what we were trying to stop doing. To talk of drugs in this way, it wasn't healthy, it was with a sense of pining and nostalgia, somewhere that encouraged the old bad behavior. He told me of using water from the toilet to shoot up with in a public bathroom. I'd assumed we'd all done that, put the needle into the toilet in a bathroom stall and drawn up water to shoot into our arms.

I was scared that Jim Olson would try to kill me. Cliff was sure he would lose his job and never be trusted. I didn't want to go back to San Francisco and Cliff was afraid of his brother. We talked shit about the other people in our ward and Cliff told me about the time he'd tried to kill himself. There was a sadness, how he told it, like a missed opportunity that he mourned.

Couples weren't allowed to stay in the same room and someone from our group objected to the two of us being in the room we were in, together and gay. We held hands to fuck with the others but it wasn't like that, we were just best friends. The clarity of getting sober was a space we'd earned together, there was a sense of pride that was emboldening.

There were cigarettes and promises and confessions and situations fraught with suggestions of celebrities, and I learned to hate Los Angeles all over again. Passenger vans drove us to off-site meetings, "Cannonball" was on the radio. There were twenty of us in that hospital who were getting clean together. My dad came to family day and we all sat in a circle. He told the group about his cancer and how he wished he had the chance the rest of us did. But he didn't. He was going to die soon. He did.

Three weeks later in a big hospital bed in the den of our family house.

I'd been responsible for his morphine drip. I was out of rehab and was the one in the family put in charge of administering the morphine drip. Me. It's true I was best versed at the intake of the drug and how it worked and stopped working, but still. My judgment in the matter was obviously questionable. In the end I was scared I'd given him too much and killed him. He was dying anyway. That sounds insane to say but there's a place of acceptance in the face of death that's comfortably unorthodox.

The windowed doors were open out to the back porch and the green and the stillness of the yard were coming into the room. My three sisters and my mom and I leaned in at his last breath. His passing at that point had become so predictable and expected. My mom looked at us all, his hand in hers as he passed, and said, "Let's go to Mexico."

We laughed at it. We were able to laugh as he died. We were crying and laughing at the same time. Like later when a big horse, his horse, crossed in front of the car we all sat in in South Dakota. We were there burying his body, months later. The horse was one that he'd rode when he went on a trip with his cowboy friends. The huge black horse stopped in front of our car and shit.

"Dad," Elizabeth said.

My father was hilarious.

We'd gone and looked at his dead body right after he'd passed in a holding tank at the mortuary in Los Angeles. His face was taut and stretched and his skin tone was yellow and gray. My cousin put a rosary in his casket. I started to write things down because I couldn't remember a thing. I kept a detailed diary and notations of what happened and what I said at the funeral service and who was there. I don't know where that diary is, I wrote it all down and never saw it again.

The funeral was in a huge Catholic church that we'd gone to as a family. When I was little and my father wore a suit and my sisters all matched. There are massive, over-sized chandeliers, eight of them, four on each side of the church, hanging high above the pews. I'd always noticed that my father would steer our family to a place not di-rectly under one of those chandeliers. In my child head, he didn't want us crushed in case one fell. It dawned on me at the funeral that that gesture of protection was now gone.

Brian Hoye told me when we were little about the time at eight o'clock mass that the huge cross with Jesus up front had fallen down and Jesus got up and righted it, put it back on the wall. We had been at nine thirty mass and the mess had been fixed and cleaned up by then. We'd go to that church in the mornings as children during Lent for the early mass and walk to school from there. We'd do that so we could miss out on the first fifteen minutes of classes. I'd sit in the pews with my friends, we'd paw at each other and make small noises with our mouths, and I'd hear my mother clear her throat from somewhere in the church, watching me. The clearing of her throat was so distinctive, like a beacon, a shout-out in the silence of the service. She had pinched me in those pews when I was younger and acting out, until the time I said to her, "Don't pinch me," audibly, in a speaking voice, very rational. It embarrassed her and she never did it again. Like the time you hear about from boys who have been smacked by their fathers; the time they stood up to him and hit back was the last time it happened. Only my father never hit me.

I continue to write things down but I still can't remember them. What . . . I'm to look things up when I forget, is that it? Like we do on our phones now to prove a point? I'll try. There were those pews, the chandeliers, a slow walk to the pulpit to talk about my father, standing room only, Courtney was there, the stenographer from my father's office, Gerri with the long-long fingernails, my father's friends I hadn't met from out of town. There was food, the doorbell rang with meals in bowls and plastic containers and instructions on how to warm things up. It felt like vacation and it felt like the end of my days.

The air and my vision and the smells and the sounds of everything were too loud and crisp. It was all painfully vivid, every edge sharp. I started to dream, crazy dreams about famous friends and failure. Speculative beginnings with disastrous endings. Real became important and priorities came into play. I hated the situationals, my boyfriend, my band, I resented responsibility and sneered at hints of ambition. Everything was just so loud and honest. I kept hoping for things to matter, nothing ever did. There was hope and there was patience and there was honesty and then there was nothing in the world that mattered.

Cliff died the next week. We had been inseparable after rehab and were in the throes of doing ninety meetings in ninety days. We were getting through it together, but he never stopped talking about seeing his dealer's car in the driveway where he used to score. He brought it up constantly. Drugs were still being sold, junkies were still lining up, nothing had stopped, and there were options and opportunities at every juncture. I'd pick him up in my

family car for the meetings and we'd hold hands sometimes, a reference to our time in the hospital. There was a
comfort to our chemistry, an honesty that was only ours.

I'd called him a dozen times and left a lot of messages
before his mother called me back and told me that he'd
overdosed. Her name was Mary, like my mother. She and
I became really close. I don't know if his dying was inten-
tional or an accident. It's usually accidental at that point.
The body isn't used to the amount of drugs that it used to
receive, and when you do that amount again after being
clean for a while, it's always too much. We'd known that
though. It's how most ODs happen. It was basic junkie
know-how. Cliff definitely knew that, so yeah, maybe it
was on purpose that he died. He may have taken his life.

I felt his bones on a beach, we all took a handful of
ash. It made me sick. My body's reaction to holding him
dead and charred was to throw up. There was nowhere
to hide, I removed myself from the circle on the sand and
took three steps away from the group and vomited. A girlfriend of a friend who'd been standing next to me put her
hand on my shoulder and I smiled very small and grate-
fully, my fingers at my lips. I rejoined the circle and those
who looked at me did so with the same small smile, the
one of knowing and understanding, of sadness and sym-
pathy, of an uncomfortableness that was easier to silence
through. Touching his remains and knowing they were
bones and burnt flesh in my hand had been too much.
The suggestion of touching a friend in that way after their
passing doesn't seem wrong, and I wondered as we stood
at the edge of the water in this celebration of life what
Native Americans do when their loved ones pass. I'd like
to follow their lead.

Ashes, ashes, remnants, remains, the notion is obscene and barbaric, how even was it ever first discussed? "I've got an idea, let's burn her." And someone, her family most likely, said yes.

My mother had been in a jar for over a year when we took her to the Badlands and put her memory to rest at the local cemetery in Wall, South Dakota, next to my father. We took the jar out at sunset and drove up into the Badlands with so many of us, three sisters, nine nieces and nephews, Joey. We were spread out, dispersed casually, the younger ones up on a perch, some of us loping behind, lazy and resigned to the moment. When we set the ashes free, we all smelled it immediately. It was undeniable to anyone who knew her. Her perfume, the smell of it, gardenias, was everywhere instantly. The sun was dying behind a hill and the terrain was odd and prehistoric as her smell swirled about us in a last hurrah, a goodbye.

34
··········

eath and Dying. It was a class somewhere, I don't
know where from; either my sister took it and
I heard that phrase or I had a similar class in my high
school and never went. Why would anyone? Death and
Dying. Put your finger in your ear then smell it. Floss your
teeth and smell that floss. We are all decaying and death
is everywhere.

San Francisco came to life and sparkled in its shit. It
had been asleep for as long as I had. The village went off
when I went back to it. So many things I'd forgotten or
hadn't noticed. The city literally stung my face, the gray
cold air, damp with its stupid fog, its visuals too loud and
clarified, my headspace was cracked and spun. Those heroes from the village were still there. The walking man
in the red socks, the old-lady twins, the screaming man
at the Polk Street cable cars, a cast of idiots and geniuses
existing together in those years barely knowing what a
computer was.

I'd moved back to my house above the Castro to start
again, amid the residue and the fallout and the leftovers.
Coming down the stairs from my bedroom to the bathroom, there wasn't a bathroom upstairs, and the sun
wasn't up. I already had a sense of the promise of the day,
being sober and attuned to the walls of my house and the

outside of the world before things began. The lights from the ceiling were dimmed and there was Jim, the boyfriend not yet sober, on the sofa, nodded out with foil and drugs on his lap. He'd moved out and we weren't being together but he still had a key to my house and a way to get in. I went to him and picked up the foil, put it close to my face, and smelled it. The smell of damage and burn and he stirred and looked up at me. It would have been easy to get right back into it. An invitation to what we'd been hung there between us as I stood in my briefs holding the sheet of burnt foil in my hand. I wanted it and didn't care, both. Just because I'd stopped didn't mean that anyone else had.

Like a balloon popping, once it was a big voluminous bulb of color and then, just like that, it's a sad and paltry carcass. Within minutes he was gone, disappeared, and I only saw him once more. I'd gone back months later to the studio apartment we once shared and banged on the door till he let me in. His ankles had swollen up huge. Somehow that seemed connected to the pints of ice cream, empty cartons surrounding him on a futon. He was going on about the pureness of the flavor of vanilla, just like him. How it was truly life's *one* exotic flavor. I knew better than to argue and I sat by him quietly and tried not to breathe. His death was a mystery to me for a long time. He'd been living with his sleeping bag under the Golden Gate Bridge but he wasn't homeless.

I went to Seattle to try to turn things around, the idea of it, the intent, the notion was absurd in retrospect but at the same time it was optimistic and compassionate and hopefully helpful. Because I'd gotten sober and I was someone Kurt respected, Courtney thought I could change things. My presence, just being there. It felt good to be thought of in that way.

She called me and promised to pay for my ticket and then never did. The two of them had bought a big estate and Frances was toddling and the script on what marriage and family in a modern world could be was being rewritten and flipped, right then, right there, on the side of a lake in that sad logging town. A fax machine that never stopped spewing, boxes of cheap sugar cereal, rotating dead flower arrangements, no spoons in the kitchen drawer, a Volvo. I was of no help to anyone but myself. It felt sycophantic. I'm not sure what that word means. There were drugs and drugs and drugs and I coasted through some days there situationally. I didn't want to get high. The drugs were nothing more to me than a bad breath from yesterday morning.

There was a crew there. Cali, Rene, Dylan, Mark, people who facilitated and really were just living their best lives. Cali who I called Cai because Frances did. I knew him vaguely from Jabberjaw, the club in Los Angeles, he'd booked bands there and became Frances's nanny before Amra. I'd played guitar there in that club loud with Kurt and maybe Eric, from Courtney's band. I told myself we were starting a band when we were all high and delusional.

The rotating yes people in Seattle were abundant, but there were suits too who would drop in and check on things. Mostly unannounced, like caseworkers with an agenda. Older people who were involved in the money side of things. We knew not to trust the suits, the rest of us being still kids. The yes kids among us said yes because it was easy and that's what friends sometimes did. I'm still friends with all of them, the ones who are alive.

On a whim and a stab at normalcy, Courtney and Kurt and I took the family Volvo at night to see the Coen brothers movie, the one that features a Hula-Hoop in an Americana backdrop. Kurt drove and we kind of banged our way down the driveway, knocking the side wall as we left the property. Courtney was scared Kurt would bolt and she wanted me to sit on the other side of him in the theater so he wouldn't. Kurt between us in the dark theater, fidgeting and captive. There were things I didn't understand about their relationship. When I left the house, days later, Kurt was in the upstairs bathroom with Dylan and a spoon, almost spilling the dope but never quite. Junkies are so good at that. I know I was. The dope is the priority and no matter how far down your nodding head will fall, holding the spoon steady and level and not spilling took precedence. I kissed him goodbye on the lips and he said, "Mmmmmm, you kiss me like a man, boy."

They call it a pink cloud or a pink bubble, something pink. The optimistic window that opens after getting sober. A reference maybe to rose-colored glasses or however that saying goes. I had optimism, I had hope, I was aiming for a direction in the distance that was vague. There was still fog in the village, shapes were blurred, landmarks were obscured, it was best to keep my vision focused on the point directly in front of me. Or else squint to get a more peripheral view. What now? Make copies of keys? Learn to cook? To balance a checkbook? All of it felt pointless.

A week after I left Seattle there was an intervention and soon after that Kurt shot himself in the back house. Courtney called and then it was immediately everywhere.

The news and the phone was ringing and the sting of it was like a smack to the face. I flew immediately back. She offered to pay for my flight and again never did.

Over and over in the world of trauma, people don't know what to say. There's a politeness and a reverence that feels like it could be right, but that's just youth. As young children, we hardly knew what to do. Walking back into the house at Lake Washington there was a pall of silence in the foyer. I'd taken a taxi from the airport and there were clumps of us on the front stairs and in chairs, together in couples, not knowing what to do or say. Joe Mamá and Patty were there and we clung to each other in the house for over a week. It was tiptoes, that's what it was, people not sure how to act but feeling that tiptoes were a good start.

A bubble in time, a placeholder in space. The gravity on the other side of hope we'd had for who Kurt was and the prospects he represented. It was a sinkhole of despair, an unfathomable wallop we all saw coming from the corner of an eye. Inevitable, so cruel. The together had never felt more important. The crowding of gestures and sympathies, what we were feeling, the exchanges of who we were and what we were going through, the clasping of hands, eye contact in the face of loss. Nothing had felt more real. Nothing had been more real.

Courtney was wailing from her bed on the phone surrounded by candles burning and trays and spilling teacups, expensive dirty sheets and frills and lavender and flowers being brought up to her room. Magazines and overflowing ashtrays. There were a lot of pills and sedatives happening because there honestly just had to be. The magnitude of his life, the realness of who he was, the love of a partner and the father of a child. We tried to keep Frances away from the TV, she'd see "Heart-Shaped Box," which was practically on a loop, and say "Dada." Young people aren't fit to deal with the drama of all that. I don't mean Frances, I mean the rest of us.

Hundreds of people came through and sent flowers and I tried to keep track to send thank you notes but it became pointless. Siouxsie and Budgie sent flowers. I wrote it down, but what even to do with that?

We went to the funeral home and his face was like my father's had been. Stretched and tight and puckered in a semi-smile. Laid out in a casket. Courtney was hysterical, in a grief frenzy, and straddled his body, got on top of him in the casket, cut a lock of hair from his head, and pushed it into my hand.

Joe and I slept in a kids' room upstairs in twin beds and whispered at night. We were both sober and gay. Patty was as well. Kind of. She was and she wasn't. With the drugs, not the gay, but she wasn't sleeping there. She'd spent nights at my house in San Francisco coming off drugs and I'd unintentionally locked her in the basement when she kicked. She peed in the backyard. It was my mother's favorite story. I'd met Patty in France, at a festival that Hole was playing, in a backstage room. She'd replaced Caroline as drummer in Hole and she was lesbian. We knew of each other before we met, like an arranged marriage. She was the first queer musician friend I'd made and we became immediately close, intentionally and intensely.

Patty showed us Dyke-Ki-Ki Beach across the street from the house in Seattle. It was a dyke beach and walking there, even without Courtney, there were paparazzi. The security team walked with us and told us to keep things down when we spoke out in the yard of the house. They'd found microphones that reporters had thrown over the fence to try to listen in on what was going on.

I never went to the back house where he'd shot himself, but there was a fence between it and the park where kids were camped out with acoustic guitars and blankets and candles. Courtney would go out to them. It was like that everywhere. Long-haired kids in flannels and jeans and rips and tears through the back fence, mourning as far as the eye could see. Kurt's family came every day and checked in with Courtney. Brianne, Kurt's younger half sister, hated me and I can't remember why. She'd laid herself out on a bench in the backyard and covered herself in flowers. His mom, Wendy, was spun and supportive and scared like a reindeer. Things were funny when maybe they shouldn't have been. Kim, his sister, I loved.

There was a memorial service at some huge place in Seattle, Kim and Kelley Deal, so many out-of-context friends, hushed and awkward in ill-fitting suits. I followed Kim and Kelley out of the service and we smoked cigarettes in front when Kurt's manager took the stage. Not Janet who we kind of loved. Danny someone. I don't remember why we hated him. It felt reasonable and legitimate to pinpoint anger at a situation. There was confusion. There were no reasons and no explanations for any of it. Drugs was just a blanket excuse and a vaguery. What had happened was real but also a story being told, a fable. That's what it was like, it unfolded like a slow fairy tale. Big big pages with illustrations and words with letters large enough for children to read and understand. I can smell that book, it's recognizable, the spine of it is cracked and threadbare, having been read again and again, its edges, the corners showing themselves and their history.

Courtney insisted on going with Kat to the outdoor service at the huge park in Seattle after the funeral service. There were thousands of children. Kat was one of the oldest friends, in my tier. There weren't that many of us. Joe. Me. Kat.

Kat and Courtney were a spectacle. They walked there through the hordes and hugged children and burned candles and smoked cigarettes and led sing-alongs with acoustic guitars. There's no reasoning or explanation for how we deal with grief. Whatever works. None of us criticized the behavior or the acting out or the screaming on the phone or the tantrums or the drugs or the fits of rage and wallows of mourn. All of it was pertinent and poetically viable, excusable, relatable, understandable.

35
·········

I returned to San Francisco spent and anxious, wanting attention or consolation, any stimulation that would make me feel different. I fantasized about taking Frances with me and raising her in San Francisco, buying a stroller. It never stopped raining in the village and there were leaks in my ceiling in four different places. I'd move the pots and the buckets and another drip would start. I stopped trying to keep up and just watched the drips from the sofa.

Increments of fifteen minutes I'd count. I'd replay things that had happened to me and tally up the minutes I'd been alive. With a calculator in my hand, I'd figure out the number of minutes because it was a definitive and irrefutable number that couldn't be argued or challenged. The hundreds of conversations with people who were dying or were close to death haunted me and I'd go over and over what we'd shared as I tried to sleep. All of us, none excluded, were on the verge of losing everything. I'd developed an arsenal of tools that pushed me in the direction of leading with the literal and the blatant. I didn't have the patience to spend on impertinent casualties. I could only deal with conversations in terms of the up-front and real and sincere. There was no time for superfluousness. I'd begin interactions with strangers immediately and inappropriately at the heart of matters. The first question I'd ask, "What hurts?"

Grief and that level of intense engagement are exhausting. I'd been in it for so long. To sit and stare. At nothing. To do something methodical that I could repeat. Something inconsequential. A physical object I could flick with my thumb or my forefinger. Something that wouldn't give or move or change. It would just go back to where it was before I flicked it, where I could flick it again. Make it something that wouldn't matter, make it something that had no effect on anything, the world, the state of my head, my purpose.

The loss and the violence of it catapulted the grief into a different realm. Guns, dope, cancer. Bullets, needles, disease. The aggression of the weapons put me under attack. Kurt's head, blown apart. His hair and scalp I'd touched with my hands had shattered and blown out from the bullet. Scraps of skull. Cliff gone blue with a needle in his arm, behind a locked door, smelling as he rotted in the days before his body had been found. My father's yellow stretched skin laid out in a coffin and the color of his beautiful blue eyes fading to gray. The physical attributes of death, there was no arguing these facets, brutal and profound as they were. There was no escaping the threat of death and I didn't feel safe. At every turn I'd jump, jittery in crowds, expecting to be attacked. Out of the closet in the throes of trauma, losing my hair and having no love, that rule of threes was pummeling my head into oblivion.

Sitting and mourning in the house at the top of the Castro, the irony wasn't lost on me. My body was shook. I was physically inept. Lights were bright and scared me. Loud noises were disturbing. For months. Every corner I turned spooked me. Everything swam in the realm of the hammer that would drop. The anticipation of the scare in a movie.

People got too close. Conversation was too loud and pointless. I didn't notice the weather. I had night sweats. Music was shrill. Stairs were only an invitation to fall. I had to remind myself to wash. All I could relate to was Sinéad. My friends tiptoed around me respectfully, it was clear I wasn't right. I tried therapy and cried when the therapist told me she was a lesbian.

On the streets, in the village, I was rattled and sensitive, unapproachable. Eye contact with others was clumsy, misguided, nervous, and shifty, but I liked myself in the mirror and I'd hold my gaze for long breaths after barely brushing my teeth. I'd return to the house after leaving to make sure the stove was off, the candle thoroughly extinguished. I had an infection in my mouth from a tooth and was sure it was AIDS. I didn't trust myself and doubted the steps I'd take to create and move forward.

Losing things implies they're gone. The absence of things that once were. I think often of the things gone missing. They're in a specific place. It's not like they don't exist anymore. They are somewhere, just not with me. The drugs were gone and so was Jim. But drugs were still being sold, the dealer was still delivering on her motorcycle, she'd still be delivering to Jim. Jim was gone but he was still in the studio apartment we'd lived in, doing drugs. The physicalness of the loss was real, as real as it gets. The loss of love was real and I was alone. Just because behavior is bad doesn't mean it's not missed. The loss of my life was lonely and my physical body was empty.

At my optimistic best I strived for a better we, for

someplace I could be proud of. I wanted to recast the Village People, to modernize the concept and make it more relevant. A butcher and a postman, getting rid of the cowboy, keeping the Native American. Little mattered in the end that wasn't close to my heart of intentions, and little changed in a place that had stopped.

I took a swim-enhancement class at the downtown YMCA to work on my crawl. There was a new method where you pull yourself more on your side as you stroke, not on your stomach. I was intent on enhancing my freestyle. A large sterile body of water with lanes, absolute direction. Swimming between those lanes in a straight line, back and forth, back and forth. The smell of clean, of chlorine, anesthesia. I recognize the poetry in my direction only as I write it now. The need for parameters.

There was an older woman in the pool named Kathy who worked with teenagers with Down syndrome. She talked me into swimming in the bay. We discussed it in the shallow end as we waited to swim our lap for the evaluating instructor. There was something in her eye, Kathy in the pool in her one-piece, her goggles propped on her forehead, indentations around her eyes. I was so tired, she was not. There was a club in front of Ghirardelli Square near Fisherman's Wharf called Aquatic Park where people swam and rowed boats. It was very old, before me, before the hippies, outside of anything I'd ever known. We drove there, she in her truck, me following on my motorcycle, to check it out. It was a mix of hooligans, fire workers, blue collar, East Bay, free spirit, but successful Ivy League spice, thoroughly confusing. We learned to row the rowboats and swam there every day.

I'd ride my motorcycle to the bay at high tide when

the water was coming in, coming in from the ocean. If the tide was leaving the bay, ebbing, the water was dirty and people complained of getting sick when they swam. When the tide was flowing, coming into the bay from the ocean, it was clean. We'd meet and walk, five or six of us, far away from the club, and jump into the bay from a wharf somewhere and swim with the tide back to the club. We followed the tide book like a bible and learned to ride it when it came in.

We would swim far. On New Year's Day when the water was forty-seven degrees we would take boats out to Alcatraz, jump into the bay, and swim back. I breathe on both sides, turn my heads both directions, a breath every three strokes, so I'd see the Golden Gate Bridge on one breath, the Bay Bridge on the next, headed to the city from the island. The swim would take almost an hour and we'd end it in a small wooden sauna in the boathouse.

The water was healing but the fix was not immediate. It was hard to trust myself. I swam every day but I'd come home on my motorcycle and accidentally leave the motor running, parked in the garage with the door closed. A neighbor would check in to see I wasn't killing myself. It never seemed to be me, the one we were all so concerned about.

My head and my hands and my body weren't working together. I could look at my fingers but couldn't make them do what they needed to do. I had stopped moving forward but the village around me continued on like a tedious, unstoppable machine that churns out useless things, one at a time, misshapen and original. The band members came to my house and we all sat on the floor. I pulled at a loose gray piece of the carpet and listened to the conversation. It was like I wasn't there. The attempt felt remotely brotherly and I was reservedly and politely given permission to not engage in the writing and the project we were expected to create. I didn't want to not do it and I didn't want to do it.

I could have talked myself into being able to do my part. I could add the pretty on top of the heavy, but the whole of it, the thesis, the core was awry and unsettling. The perspective, the voice, the message was askew. What we'd championed, the mix, the diversity, the different flavors, all of these were confusing to me in a way they hadn't been before. The elements that propelled what we'd done and gotten famous for felt complicated. More than anything I needed simple and honest and from the heart, and I wasn't able to find that in the mix.

One voice as opposed to a cacophony. A tone compared to a barrage. An expression and not a posture. The volume didn't matter. A whisper or a scream. Gravitating toward simple and perfunct, quiet or with multitudinal wallop. I didn't know what I wanted but it was clear what I didn't.

Trauma and overwhelmption, is that a word? I evaluated and reevaluated and explored memories as if I were reading a book about someone else. If only it was someone else's story and not mine. The antics and trouble I'd grown up getting into struck me as backhanded and dishonest. The mindset I'd grown accustomed to relying on, snickering behind my hand and throwing things off buildings, it confused me. Like the ceiling over my head, sadness was a soak and a wetness I couldn't stop the creeping of.

There was also a loss of love. There was sex I continued to throw myself into, but the interludes were mechanical and loveless, there was never a connection. If a name was mentioned I did my best to forget it, faces the same. Mechanical and desperate, alone and maniacal, devoid of loving a someone who I'd respect enough to love me.

36

....

I met Will in the space of time between sick and dead and better. He'd gone on a couple of dates with Cliff before he died, when we were first out of rehab. He had just gotten clean too. I'd seen him down beyond us at the end of a line of seats at a meeting, sitting by himself. Cliff had whispered in my ear about what he was wearing and I'd leaned forward and looked down the row at him. They'd had sex at that point. Will was so handsome and so well put together, keys clutched in his lap, staring straight ahead, well aware we were talking about him. His outfits were coordinated in the most unorthodox way and he spoke honestly, intuitively, with an insight of breadth and wonder that was childlike. He stuttered astutely and confidently.

I took Will home after we spread Cliff's ashes to meet my sisters. He and I shared a commonplace of people and music and flavors we appreciated together, but we didn't know each other that well. We both had nowhere to go. I'd earned respect from my sisters by getting sober and being present. It was early evening and there was a baby doll on the counter in the kitchen. I don't know where she came from, that baby doll, but Will impulsively bent down and kissed her on the lips. Elizabeth leaned on the counter in her casual style and pulled the doll by the leg to herself and kissed her as well. We all kissed that baby doll.

It's much easier to start a band than it is to keep one afloat. New things are shinier and have an easier go. A first-time look is going to achieve better results and that is the sad stage of us as a people. It's an ugly discourse to the notions of loyalty, history, nostalgia, stick-aroundedness, but there it is. We're attracted to things that are new.

Will had never been in a band, he was just learning how to play the guitar. Lynn had never stepped away from the drums, Jone had never played bass, I had never played guitar, and I'd never sung before. The freshness and the challenge of what it would take for us to write songs would create a vision and a direction of honor and integrity.

Lynn was a drummer and one of my best friends, one I'd wrestled with drunk and at shows. Our agenda was simple, we aimed to spurn a project of beginners. We asked Jone to join us, she had been in the Wrecks with Lynn when they were teenagers, and I asked Will to come up to the village from Los Angeles and help make things happen. Our premise was that honesty and purity would come from novices. It was all I was capable of. Creating sounds and melodies, the sharing of an audible voice, the exercise of waving a flag that spoke, it's inherent in me, the need and the propulsion to share who I am and what I'm going through.

Starting Imperial Teen was easy. We leaned into simple. The only craft we focused on was one of honesty. Honesty and cheek but honesty for certain. We bonded over the choices that we made and Lynn and Will and Jone became my first chosen family. One that functioned. The other band had so famously operated on dysfunction, the dysfunction became a calling card. Imperial Teen was built from a place of trust and camaraderie that was poignant and heartfelt and emotionally charged. We looked after each other and coddled ourselves like siblings after the death of a parent or the loss of a pet. I needed more than anything to feel safe and taken care of, so I turned that nurturing part of myself on the world.

I brought over $400 to a guitar shop on lower Mission Street to find a guitar to play and write with, I didn't own one. I'd only strummed an acoustic guitar on a lap. I knew PJ Harvey played a hollow-body with MXR distortion so that's where I was going. I found a Gretsch guitar up on the wall in the back of the music shop that spoke to me. I looked at it up on the wall and it looked like me. It was brown and simple with only one pickup, not a show-off, a humble pedestrian, a sturdy dog. When I went back to the front of the store to ask someone to help me take the guitar down off the wall, all of the staff were lying down on the ground on their stomachs. I thought it was a game, San Francisco was so unpredictable. A man grabbed me from behind and put a gun to my head. He put me on the floor and kept the gun at my head for a long time and held my neck and went through my pockets. I didn't panic, I went to a very calm place. I wasn't fazed, I was thinking about me and the gun and my head blown up and it was all just okay. I worried about the other guys on the floor, the store owner, the other guy who worked there, a few customers, and I felt bad for our families, how they'd mourn. I thought about my funeral and who would be there, the music that would be played. I'd always asked for that song "Popcorn," I hoped that wish would be obliged.

It was restful on the ground, lying down, being silent, in the midst of activity, peaceful. I felt for the men who were robbing us. I thought of their families and expectations of lovers and secrets that they shared. I wondered who they'd tell of this exploit. Would it be mentioned with pride or shame? I thought of pride and my father and if he'd be proud of me on the ground, holding my own. I lay there on the floor and I cried. Not out of fear, I wasn't scared, I cried for the sadness of the world. My face was a mess, I was sobbing and the dirt from the floor was mixed into the tears on my cheeks as we counted. The men with the guns told us to count to 100 when they left the store. We did it together, out loud, no one cheated or went fast in the counting, we just lay there on our stomachs and counted together. I didn't have to explain my tears to the rest as we got up.

For Imperial Teen's first attempt at songwriting, we didn't have microphone stands. I took the guitar, the Gretsch I'd bought from the shop, and we set up instruments in a space using towels for some reason to hold our microphones in place. Towels, tied and held in place. That seemed appropriate and we spoke and laughed about it later and often. In that crippled space, the songs fell out of us. Much of it was Will who is a genius. He opens his mouth and magic, glorious ladybirds come out. We started with our singing and added the chemistry of the four of us and it was undeniable. From the start. We wrote songs over the span of a couple weeks to prepare for a show we'd committed to way before we'd been ready.

Will and I sat in a café together and called what we were doing Word Week. We wrote the lyrics that we'd sing. Lyrics that were real and pertinent to us. I sang about death, about Kurt, about my father, about drugs, about being gay, about anger and how it felt. I sang about struggle and hope and failure and lies. We sang about each other and who we were to each other.

The songs came from that place. We recorded them at a really early stage of the band. We'd initially set out to find a producer who had no game. Our first idea was Naomi Campbell. A supermodel producing an album was genius to me. It was something I liked to say aloud: "Naomi Campbell is going to produce." The connection with Naomi wasn't there, we didn't have a way to get in touch with her, so we reached out to Kelley Deal. Not Kim Deal. Kelley Deal. When I asked Kim for Kelley's number, she assumed I was confusing the twins. She was like, "No, I'm Kim. Kelley is the other one." But we wanted the other sister, the one who'd basically just learned her instrument, to produce. There was a story about Kelley leaving her job as an analyst in the defense industry to join her sister in the band. I don't know whether or not it was true, but the point was that she was a beginner. In the end she didn't do it, there had been a heroin arrest I'm choosing not to remember. We got our friend Steve McDonald to record us. He had never produced anything and Jone and I loved him from forever. His band Redd Kross came from a family place. He had started a band with his older brother when he was eleven and his brother was thirteen. That fit with where we were going and we felt safe with him.

We recorded in San Francisco in under a week with Steve and another engineer man who had little hands. We had a record's worth of songs. I'd never sung and sometimes I'd overdramatize and transform weirdly into a sort of Southern belle. Hearing what I was capable of behind a microphone scared me. What I wasn't capable of was scary too, but not like I'd thought. My limitations were profound but inspirational. I liked what I wasn't able to do and worked with the vulnerability of not achieving what I aimed for.

37

....

The first record I heard as a boy, the one that I pulled out of a sleeve and put on a turntable, was *Bridge Over Troubled Water*. I sang "El Condor Pasa" into a tape recorder that I'd found in a drawer. My father used it to dictate things into so he wouldn't forget. It was half the size of a phone book, the record button was red.

Some months later I was at my grandparents' house in Wall, South Dakota. I worked as a table cleaner in the diner of their tourist attraction for the summer, I wasn't older than nine. We would come back to the house in the middle of the day and sit down at a big table together. They called that meal dinner, and then the one after it, at night, was called supper. Breakfast was breakfast but dinner was always an afternoon sit-down in the wooden room with the player piano that's now in my garage. There was a woman named Frances who wore an apron and cousins who were there like me, visiting and working for the summer. I'd pushed the sweeping side of a broom into one cousin's face during a fight we'd had in the backyard of the store and she sat across from me, her face covered in pricks, she hadn't told. My grandpa was at the head of the table. My grandma sat at the other end, she didn't stop moving, fussing, shuffling, she smelled like money, the paper kind. There was an older cousin I looked up to who scared me. Patty Quinn, he didn't like to be called that. He bred rabbits in hutches that he kept under a carport around the side of his house. He lived next door to my grandparents with his brothers and sisters and sometimes rode a horse.

The cassette had come in the mail, my parents sent it, they sent it to my grandparents. I had made it for me but they played it at the table that afternoon as we ate. My voice was high, I sounded like a sister, not a Garfunkel. Even my grandma looked embarrassed at the sound of the cassette. It wasn't just me singing on the tape, I had emoted and crooned to affect. No words at the supper table were said. My cousin with the pricked face looked at me scared and the one with the bunnies snickered and chuckled into his food.

That first experience of hearing myself, experiencing myself honestly, recorded by a device with no filter, a straightforward depiction that there was no arguing with, no room for error, was horrifying. I didn't know gay shame at the time but I'd grown up to know that the way I sounded was wrong. The lilt and the emoting that played out from the cassette were like a string of dirty words I'd been warned not to use. This look in the mirror, this pivotal reflection of fractured concrete precision, there was no arguing. A boy who sounded like a sister. A sound of disfigurement, a telltale heart on a sleeve, a picture of poetry that not only broke the rules of gender stereotypes in that Midwest dining room but fell flat as the family listened. It took years to right this judgment.

Standing in a recording studio with headphones, one ear on, one ear off, looking away from the glass of the control room where everyone watched. Singing, the memories and the damage of a boy at a young age don't go away. They're there, first and foremost, guiding me, shaming me, pushing me to be who I was, who I am. It was work to make it right, to harness the inner sissy, to not be affected by the disgust of self-shame and turn it into a tool the way God fucking intended. To give emotion, to give truth, to give the side of me that was shunned but ultimately provident to the apex of my core. To share, to give, to perform, to create from a headspace of self-acceptance was the answer to the riddle of my life. Among my people, in a comfort zone, I earned and owned who I was and sang from my heart. These were the givings of not only Imperial Teen but the fruits of my people, my family, roots I was becoming familiar with.

Imperial Teen became us as a family, the four of us and our world. Our words, our neuroses, our working through the course of each other, our friendship, it all became our delivery. There was no denying who we were and how we loved each other. Siblings. We looked out for each other, cheered each other on, and made room for our mistakes.

Will is magic. He is a passionate hyena lady singing the blues. Jone is a marvel and a master of a mix of so many things. We called her GrabBag for a while, alluding to her variety of knows. Lynn is a rage and a storm of passion, strength, and woman, empowered sexualization of performance and execution, like the Raquel Welch character in that Stone Age movie. Our sound reflected who we were, our operation became our art, our ethic become our product, and we connected with people who gravitated toward realness in that way.

As we wrote songs and became who we were, we took

photos of ourselves in a mall at a family photo stand in front of a backdrop of balloons. We smiled and held each other, well aware of what we were doing. It wasn't all cheek or sarcasm, it felt like us. Up-front and flawed and visible, I wrote the lyrics I needed to hear myself sing. Things I wanted to hear. I sang about almost dying, being scared, resentment and anger and the aloneness I felt being gay. The point of our project was to lead with our hearts. If the heart is pure then the craft will follow, and that intention was untouchable. It feels like a platitude or a long bumper sticker as I write it and maybe that's the trick. Such an obvious notion or premise that's there all along. That thing in the house you've seen every day and finally acknowledge: *Oh. That's what that's for.*

We humbly undersold who we were. There was pride in what we did though we recognized it as ridiculous. We took a cassette of our first recordings to the free weekly magazine in San Francisco, they ran a demo-of-the-week column in their paper. The songs struck a chord in the city that we lived in and the era that we were coming out of. The village was still provincial, tiny, unto itself. People in San Francisco still read, they were versed in politics, literature, human rights, matters of the heart. There were different sides of that city and it may be wrong to portray it as specifically such. There were idiots, there were people who don't care, there was sickness, there were loafers with no intention, there were simple-minded kids who just wanted to huff and skateboard and act out. There were clearly ambitious people of the computer, poised and crouched at the cusp of what was to come. I'd honed out a space for myself that fit me. It fit all those people too, but the ones I chose to create with were like me. They were open and curious and anxious and boldened, insecure but brave, adventurous on tiptoes. Lynn. Jone. Will. We mattered mostly unto ourselves but we made a collection of songs that spoke to people like us.

In our minds, from where we sat, we had delivered a bible. Every record, every collection, is or should be an analogy of its time, a portrait of veracity that spews from a personal space. That's what we aimed for. Imperial Teen rolled into a world of anger and doubt and cover-ups and shame and shined a light. Those for whom it didn't resonate were superfluous. We owned the world.

We called our record *Seasick*, smitten with dichotomy; the queasy title that referenced the sharp and vivid quips and messages that catapulted themselves into the bright energy that was the music. It splashed effervescently at a time that had never been darker. The tone of self-expression, of owning myself, of putting the honesty forefront in a way that I hadn't, it was a new frontier for me. The whiplash threw me into a frenzy of trying to do right, and the doing of the right started to come.

Delusional gets a bad rap. I was comforted by the confusion it brought me. I was perfectly happy to be wrong, just with questions. As aware as we were of our genius, the truth was that the world wasn't ready for Imperial Teen, the world hadn't evolved as a people as such. The world wasn't ready for queer pioneers or ready for a gay rhetoric. I know that now, but as a band, as a family, we chose not to accept it. We stumbled ahead, doing what we did, taking task, writing songs, addressing wrongs, implementing ourselves. Ours was pride, it was entitlement, it was beginners' love of ourselves in the mirror.

To straddle is an art. Which circus folk, entertainers,

magicians can do it effectively? It's an act of athletes, a prowess of physical know-how. To adjust, to become something else while acknowledging the before, a tug-of-war between what I did and what I'd do. It was sudden and arresting, on the precipice of then and now. I embellish and exaggerate, certainly, 'cause what's more customary or expected than working and creating with different people? It's what we're made of as artists, what we aim for, and truthfully, what I do well: collaborating, juggling two balls at once, walking in different crowds, adjusting and smoothing the wrinkles as it works for me. At that particular time, though, so raw from tragedy and the coma of being dead for so long, all points and feelings were exaggerated.

Seasick hit all the marks. It was nominated and then won the Grammy for Best New Artist, Record of the Year, Single of the Year, and we received a Pride Achievement Award from the Gays of the World Foundation. We were recognized far and wide for our input and perspective in putting gay sentiments up front in a time when such ideas were challenged and ostracized. Applauded for taking risks and being honest among a slew and nation of lies, statues were put up in parks and our silhouettes were forged onto coins. History was created and like always I am a part as a scribe, an intuit, and a liar.

I'd lived and I'd died. I threw everything I had into the air and watched it fall. I was rooted in where I'd been but relished the thought of the merry-go-round burning. The future had never been less relevant. It is clearly a fathom and a concept that doesn't exist. It is not there and I forced myself to accept that. The breath as it plays in the present is one of loving and one worth being loved. The past as a reference, of course, it's she I adhere to and here I am. Deliverable and deliberate, pointed and exercised, alive not dead.

38

....

The fog in the village grew denser and thicker till no one could see a thing, not three feet in front of them. The smell of rot set in and all conversation stopped. A collection of elders remained but their voices were ignored as the village around them crumbled into something new. The cold white blanket, wet and heavy, smothered all that had been. The music stopped and the children died. In its place was the glorious Internet and all that it brought. The ease of life. The casual and specific luxury of getting answers with the wave of a hand. Button-down boys with their juju-bead bracelets eating peanut M&M's, strollers and strollers and half-drunk women talking loud, cars replacing bikes, eventually driving themselves. What was the point in reading or listening with your ear to the ground when the death of the village had already been decided? The only thing left to hear was the slowing of the pulse, the sporadic of a heartbeat that finally stopped. Smell and taste and tactile fruition took a backseat to a pertinence of poison in the new industry. Goodbye, fuckers. I will always hate you.

I left the village as it burned in the rearview mirror. Most of us fled in the onslaught of the suffrage, what else could we do? Stumbling in and out of love, I moved to New York and found the man and the world I'd known but didn't. There were highs, there always were, but trag-edy was always so much more prevalent, so much more potent. The rule of threes continued in the aftermath of the collapse.

My house burned down, I found my best friend hang-ing in a stairwell, Chuck overdosed on heroin.

A lunatic ran the country, a pandemic ravaged, my mother died in her bed.

There's no such thing as closure, can you imagine put-ting a date on the end of an era? I've heard that plenty of times after a punctuated something, a clarity that sums up a pinnacle of time. Like the handle coming off the ceramic mug I used every morning in my third year of high school.

"Well, that's the end of an era," my mother smirked, as I bewildered up at her, trying to make sense of the bro-ken handle in my hand.

In my stubborn way, of course, it wasn't. I saved the handle that broke and put it in a drawer of special things and continued to use the mug despite its morph. It hon-estly *was* the end of an era, some sort of era, some shift in time and memory and nostalgia that never came back. The notion of the memory would only exist in my head as the mechanics and regularity of the action stopped. If I hadn't written it down, the era wouldn't exist. My mother had been aware of it but that memory died with her so now it's only with me. Eras are personal, my eras are my own. Memories are singularly charged from a headspace that is alone and quiet and tight like a drum. Until they're shared.

There are millions of memories and moments I'll never share. My heart is in the inconsequential ones, the small punctuations of personality and rifts of roughage from children, gangs, collections of friends who laugh and speculate wildly with flair. These stories reflected aloud I strain for, I live for, and yearn to be a part of. The difficulty of death is the naked and pungent possibility that the essence of those memories go away. They leave, never shared again.

It's hard to get behind the disappearing of things, to accept that things leave. In the end they are replaced by new things and new is just ugly, an uninvited guest, an impostor with no bearings or history or know-how. Until new becomes old, I can't get on board.

A familiar worn sweater I saw on my father for so many years as he swung a golf club on the front lawn, shucking clams at a dirty outdoor sink on a camping trip, the neck of the sweater twisted and pulled as he looked back over his shoulder, reversing the car into traffic spinning wildly around us. The memories and connections to that sweater are what I live for. I want nothing more than that. The palpability of a fabric, the swaddle of a memory, a smell, stubble rubbed against me as I brush against it, keys in a jumble at the bottom of a pocket, sound everywhere but the discerning of a laugh that I know by heart, the untangling of emotions and closures and catastrophes that almost killed me, I'll never know an ending until I close my eyes.

The End

Thank you Amra Brooks, Alex Auder, Courtney Love, Frank Haines, Regina Joskow, Paul Soileau, Julie Panebianco, Lydia Lunch, Jessica Hopper, Pony Rivers, David Dunton, Johnny Temple, Johanna Ingalls, Melissa Auf der Maur, Patty Schemel, Lynn, Jone, Will, JD, Michael, Billy, Mike, Mike P, Jim, Jon, my mother, Catherine, Elizabeth, Stephanie, and Joey.